FLORENCE NIGHTINGALE AND THE CRIMEA, 1854–55

uncovered editions

Series editor: Tim Coates

Titles in the series

uncovered editions

FLORENCE NIGHTINGALE AND THE CRIMEA, 1854–55

London: The Stationery Office

First published 1855, 1856
© Crown Copyright

This abridged edition
© The Stationery Office 2000
Reprinted with permission.
All rights reserved. No part of this publication may be
reproduced, stored in a retrieval system, or transmitted in
any form or by any means – electronic, mechanical,
photocopying, recording or otherwise – without the prior
permission of the copyright owner. In the first instance write
to the Contracts and Rights Manager, The Stationery Office
Limited, St Crispins, Duke Street, Norwich NR3 1PD.

ISBN 0 11 702425 2

A CIP catalogue record for this book is available from the
British Library

Typeset by J & L Composition, Filey, North Yorkshire
Printed in the United Kingdom for The Stationery Office by
Biddles Limited, Guildford, Surrey.
TJ 000858   C30   04/00

Uncovered Editions are historic official papers which have not previously been available in a popular form. The series has been created directly from the archive of The Stationery Office in London, and the books have been chosen for the quality of their story-telling. Some subjects are familiar, but others are less well known. Each is a moment of history.

Series editor: Tim Coates

Tim Coates studied at University College, Oxford and at the
University of Stirling. After working in the theatre for a number
of years, he took up bookselling and became managing director,
firstly of Sherratt and Hughes bookshops, and then of
Waterstone's. He is known for his support for foreign
literature, particularly from the Czech Republic. The idea for
"Uncovered Editions" came while searching through the
bookshelves of his late father-in-law, Air Commodore
Patrick Cave OBE. He is married to Bridget Cave,
has two sons, and lives in London.

*The Crimean War lasted from 1854 until 1856.
It included the battles of the Alma, Inkerman,
Balaklava and the siege of Sebastopol. At the battle
of Balaklava in 1854 the famous Charge of the
Light Brigade took place.*

*The British and the French sided with the Turks to
prevent the expansion of the Russian Empire into
Persia and the Balkans. Turkey commanded the entry
into the Black Sea at Constantinople, through the
Bosphorous straits, so the British Army was shipped
from a base in Malta to Varna on the west side of
the Black Sea. It was not clear at this time whether
there would be war, which created problems for those
organising the logistics of the army on the move.*

*In August 1854 war eventually did begin and the
allied armies embarked for the Crimea with the objective
of laying siege to the Russian city of Sebastopol.
In Varna the army fell victim to a plague of cholera.
It was decided to set up hospitals on the Bosphorous
at Scutari which faces Constantinople. These hospitals
would care for the sick and the wounded who would
be shipped from the harbour at Balaklava. The journey
by boat from Balaklava to Scutari was about four
days. At Scutari there were a number of Turkish
buildings suitable for use as hospitals including a
palace and a large barrack. The hospitals were intended
to support smaller field hospitals in the Crimea at
Balaklava and other places close to the army.*

During the autumn word came back to London of severe problems that were being encountered by the army and not being reported by officers in despatches from the field. They were of all kinds; there were difficulties of supply, not only to the men but also to the huge number of horses used by the cavalry. Arrangements for sheltering and taking medical care of the soldiers were said to be terrible and many essential supplies seemed to have gone missing.

During the first six months of the campaign there were several government enquiries into what was happening. Thousands of pages of reports and statistics were compiled in an effort to take the right actions.

The press, particularly "The Times", was publishing letters from families of the men describing the appalling conditions. This embarrassed the government, but even more it irritated the army, which did not know how to cope with such open scrutiny of its activities.

These short extracts from government papers of those months are not intended to provide a history of the war or any part of it. They have been selected in order to provide a snapshot of events as they were presented to parliament. In particular they focus on the terrible disaster that was the Charge of the Light Brigade (during the battle of Balaklava) and the inadequate provisions that were made for the care of the sick and wounded, both in the field and at Scutari. The documents relating to the hospitals at Scutari include evidence of the ministry of Florence Nightingale.

Prologue

Location map

COPY of Letter from the Duke of Newcastle, the Minister for War, dated 6th December 1854, addressed to certain newspapers, respecting the publication of intelligence from the seat of war in the Crimea.

Sir,   *War Department, 6th December* 1854
I take the liberty of sending to you an extract from a private letter which I have lately received from Lord Raglan.

Many complaints have reached me from the army of the advantages conferred upon the enemy by the publication of intelligence from the seat of war, not only in letters from the correspondents of the English newspapers, but in letters written by officers to their friends at home in the spirit of confidential intimacy, and which those friends send to the newspapers, from feelings, no doubt, of pardonable vanity, but without consideration of the evil consequences to the army, and the public interests.

I feel assured that I have only to appeal to your patriotism to ensure a rigid supervision of all such letters, and an endeavour to prevent the mischief of which Lord Raglan so reasonably complains.

I am etc.

(signed)

Newcastle

Extract from the letter from Lord Raglan to the Duke of Newcastle:

I have requested Mr. Romaine to endeavour to see the different correspondents of the Newspapers, and quietly point out to them the public inconvenience of their writings and the necessity of greater prudence in future, and make no doubt that they will at once see that I am right in so warning them.

I would suggest that you should cause a communication to be made to the Editors of the daily press, and urge upon them to examine the letters they receive before they publish them, and carefully expunge such parts as they may consider calculated to furnish information to the enemy.

PART 1

The Charge of the Light Brigade at
the Battle of Balaklava, 1854

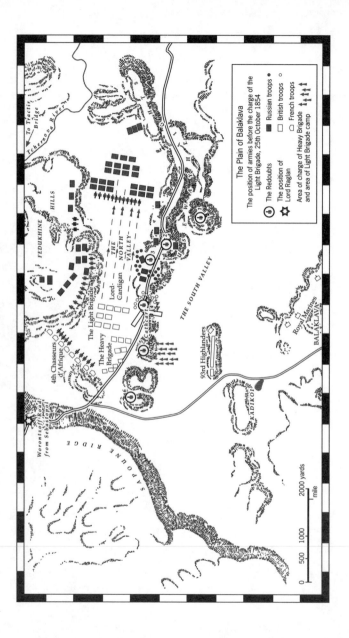

The Plain of Balaklava
The position of armies before the charge of the Light Brigade, 25th October 1854

① The Redoubts
★ The position of Lord Raglan

■ Russian troops
□ British troops
○ French troops

Area of charge of Heavy Brigade and area of Light Brigade camp

FEDIOUKHINE HILLS

To Tractir Bridge

Tchernaya River

THE NORTH VALLEY

Lord Cardigan

The Light Brigade

The Heavy Brigade

4th Chasseurs d'Afrique

THE SOUTH VALLEY

93rd Highlanders

Royal Marines

BALAKLAVA

KADIKOI

Woronzoff Road from Sebastopol

SAPOUNE RIDGE

0   500   1000   2000 yards

mile

∽∽⌒⌒∽∽

Balaklava, October 25th to November 5th 1854.
From the report of the Royal Engineers on the preparations
of the British Army before Sebastopol.

The Russians worked at their defences with zeal and
energy well worthy of the initiation, and as their
resources in guns and ammunition, as well as the
amount of labour at their command, were enormous,
they had the power of position almost to an unlim-
ited extent. Several entirely new batteries had already
been completed, and many others were in progress on
the north as well as on the south side of Sebastopol.

But we shall allude here to such works only as were opposed to the British attacks:—

In advance of the Flagstaff Bastion, and in front of the French attack, they had constructed a small battery, which much annoyed our trenches.

The Garden batteries had been completed, and 14 guns were mounted in them.

The battery across the head of the Dockyard Creek had been enlarged, and had been armed with heavy guns.

The wall connecting the proper right flank of the Redan with the Barrack Battery had been converted into a battery for heavy guns, and new batteries were being commenced on the left flank of the Redan.

The little Redan flanking the ground in front of the Malakoff had been fully armed.

In the ruins of Inkerman Castle they had likewise established a battery for heavy guns, the fire from which caused some annoyance to the outposts of the second division; and as fears were entertained that the enemy would throw shot into the camp itself, a counter battery was erected on the extreme right flank of the allied position, and some distance in advance of the Second Division camp. This battery was completed and armed on the 24th October, and by a steady attack it effectually succeeded in silencing the enemy's guns. Its position, however, was considered too far in advance to be safely guarded at night, and the battery was shortly afterwards disarmed.

The Russians now commenced to advance, and to encroach upon the allied position in every direction.

Their picquets had been greatly increased and not only were they far superior in point of numbers to those which the allies could oppose to them, but they were generally supported by field artillery even in minor skirmishes. They constantly attacked the besiegers, whenever forced to retire or pursued they rapidly withdrew, under cover of the fire from their field-pieces, to a number of small stone rifle screens. From here they were able to take a steady deadly aim at their opponents, at the same time that they themselves remained securely protected. Many casualties occurred, and the English picquets being very small had some difficulty in maintaining their position.

On one occasion, some of the enemy's riflemen advanced during the night as far as the large quarry to the immediate front of the 21-Gun battery, and on the following morning they opened a heavy fire upon the embrasures of that battery. These skirmishes were at once driven out, yet it became clear that a strong body of troops ought to be placed in advance, to prevent the enemy from surprising the besiegers at work.

A third parallel was therefore commenced at 600 yards in front of Gordon's Battery, but want of workmen, as already stated, retarded its completion for several days.

A proposition was put forward at this period, to make a strong reconnaissance to the front, completely over the Inkerman ridge, and as far as the head of harbour, and for the following reasons: the flank was at present indifferently protected; it was of great importance to strengthen it, and this could be effected by a more complete occupation of the Inkerman ridge. The troops or lodgements of the enemy on that ridge could be but imperfectly supported, and unless they had entrenched themselves, which was most likely, they might be driven off altogether.

By this proceeding the besiegers would enforce their superiority at a distance from the works of the place, and by holding the ground in advance, however feebly, they would obtain a command of all the ravines by which an enemy could ascend the plateau from the head of the harbour, and they would thus add materially to the strength of their right flank. But the British Army was considered too weak to carry out these proposals.

A considerable number of Russian troops had meanwhile collected on the banks of the Tchernaya, and on the 20th October a force of seven strong columns of the infantry, accompanied by some guns, advanced from the northside of the river, and bivouacked on the Fedukhine heights, which cover the bridge of Tractir and are on the direct road to Balaklava. From this position they made several reconnaissances towards Balaklava, retiring, however, as soon as the Turkish redoubts opened fire upon them.

By degrees this corps of observation was increased to 18 battalions of infantry, 30 or 40 guns, and a large body of cavalry, and with this force the enemy made a determined movement against the British base of operations on the morning of the 25th October.

This position, as already stated, was defended by an inner and an outer line, the former being occupied in the following manner: a small force of Marines protected the high ground which formed the extreme right of the position: to their west, and between them and Kadikoi, was a small detachment of the 93rd Regiment, while the main body of the 93rd and a battery of artillery were drawn up in front of the village of Kadikoi. Guns of position were placed along the most prominent points of this line: they were manned by the Royal Marine Artillery, and each gun had been supplied with from 150 to 200 rounds of ammunition. The total extent of this line was about three miles, and its defence was entrusted to the command of Major-General Sir Colin Campbell. The brigades of light and heavy cavalry and a troop of horse artillery were on his left, and between Kadikoi and the plateau, in order to keep up the communication with the front.

The outer line was between 2,000 and 3,000 yards in front of this inner position, and crowned the line of low eminences which extend across the plain of Balaklava from the village of Kamara to the plateau of Sebastopol. Four small redoubts, each capable of holding from 250 to 400 men, had been hastily con-structed along this line by the Turks, under the direction of Lieut. Wafman, and they were armed with seven 12-pounder iron guns. These works, being of very slight profile, were calculated to little resist a powerful attack, and they were too far to the front to be properly supported. They were manned by a force of about 3,000 Turkish troops, of whom the greater part were raw recruits and redifs (militia).

At an early hour of the morning on the 25th October large masses of Russian infantry advanced to the attack of these redoubts, and carried them, almost without opposition. The Turks were not in sufficient numbers to offer much resistance, and being quite unsupported they had to abandon their guns and retreat in haste towards Balaklava. The Russians then threw forward their numerous cavalry, supported by a powerful artillery, against the inner line; but here they met with determined and unexpected resistance. The brigade of heavy cavalry, although far inferior to them in point of numbers, advanced to the charge, and in the most brilliant manner attacked them both in front and in flank. The enemy's squadrons were put into complete disorder, and the accurate fire of artillery, and the steadiness of the 93rd Regiment, at length forced them to retire to the protection of the Turkish redoubts.

The brigade of the light cavalry now advanced, with the view of recapturing the guns which had been taken from the Turks, and through some mis-conception of orders they charged in an injudicious but very gallant manner against a heavy cross and flank fire of artillery. They were forced to retire after suffering an immense loss.

In the "Charge of the Light Brigade", which is discussed in the following correspondence, 247 men died and also more than 300 horses were killed or had to be put down.

Field Marshal Lord Raglan to the Duke of Newcastle.
Before Sebastopol 16th December 1854

My Lord Duke,
I regret to be under the necessity of forwarding to your Grace the copy of a letter which has been addressed to me by Lieutenant-General the Earl of Lucan.

When I received it, I placed it in the hands of Brigadier-General Airey, the Quartermaster General, and requested him to suggest to his Lordship to withdraw the communication, considering that it would not lead to his advantage in the slightest degree; but Lord Lucan, having declined to take the step recommended, I have but one course to pursue, that of laying the letter before your Grace, and submitting to you such observations upon it as I am bound in justice to myself to put you in possession of.

Lieutenant-General the Earl of Lucan complains that, in my despatch to your Grace of the 28th October, I stated that, "from some misconception of the instruction to advance, the Lieutenant-General considered that he was bound to attack at all hazards." His Lordship conceives this statement to be a grave charge, and an imputation reflecting seriously on his professional character, and he deems it incumbent upon him to state these facts which he cannot doubt must clear him, from what he respectfully submits is altogether unmerited.

I have referred to my despatch, and far from being willing to recall one word of it, I am prepared to declare, that not only did the Lieutenant-General misconceive the written instruction that was sent him, but there was nothing in that instruction which called upon him to attack at all hazards; or to undertake the operation which led to such a brilliant display of gallantry on the part of the Light Brigade, and unhappily, occasioning such lamentable casualties in every regiment composing it.

In his Lordship's letter he is wholly silent with respect to a previous order which had been sent him. He merely says that the cavalry were formed to support an intended movement of the infantry.

This previous order was in the following words: "The cavalry to advance and take advantage of any opportunity to recover the heights. They will be supported by infantry, which has been ordered to advance on two fronts."

The order did not seem to me to have been attended to, and therefore it was that the instruction by Captain Nolan was forwarded to him. Lord Lucan must have read the first order with very little attention, for he now states that the cavalry was formed to support the infantry, whereas he was told by Brigadier-General Airey, "that the cavalry was to advance and take advantage of any opportunity to recover the heights, and that they would be supported by the infantry," not that they were to support the infantry; and so little had he sought to do as he had been directed, that he had no men in advance of his main body, made no attempt to regain the heights, and was so little informed of the position of the enemy that he asked Captain Nolan, "Where and what he was to attack, as neither enemy nor guns were in sight?"

This, your Grace will observe, is the Lieutenant-General's own admission. The result of his inattention to the first order was that it never occurred to him that the second was in connexion and a repetition of the first. He viewed it as a positive order to attack at all hazards (the word "attack", be it observed was not made use of in General Airey's note) an unseen enemy, whose position, numbers, and composition he was totally unacquainted with, and whom in consequence of a previous order he had taken no step to watch.

I undoubtedly had no intention that he should make such an attack; there was nothing in the instruction to require it, and therefore I conceive I was fully justified in stating to your Grace what was the exact truth, that the charge arose from the misconception of the order for an advance, which Lord Lucan considered obliged him to attack at all hazards.

I wish I could say with his Lordship that, having decided against his conviction to make the movement, he did all he could to render it as little perilous as possible. This indeed, is far from the case, in my judgment.

He was told that the horse artillery might accompany the cavalry. He did not bring it up. He was informed that the French cavalry was on his left. He did not invite their co-operation. He had the whole of the heavy cavalry at his disposal. He mentions having brought up only two regiments in support, and he omits all the other precautions, either from want of the due consideration or from the supposition that the unseen enemy was not in such great force as he apprehended, not withstanding that he was warned of it by Lord Cardigan, after the latter had received the order to attack.

I am much concerned, my Lord Duke, to have to submit these observations to your Grace. I entertain

no wish to disparage the Earl of Lucan in your opinion, or to cast a slur upon his professional reputation;
but having been accused by his Lordship of having
stated of him what was unmerited in my despatch, I
have felt obliged to enter into the subject, and trouble your Grace at more length than I could have
wished in vindication of a report to your Grace, in
which I had strictly confined myself to that which I
knew to be true, and had indulged in no observations
whatever, or in any expression which could be
viewed as harsh or in any way grating to the feelings
of his Lordship.

I have etc.
(signed)
Raglan

*The following is a copy of Lord Lucan's letter to Lord
Raglan, which Raglan forwarded to the Duke of Newcastle
with his letter of 16th December 1854.*

Lieutenant-General Earl of Lucan to Field Marshal
Lord Raglan

30 *November* 1854

My Lord,
In your Lordship's report of the cavalry action at
Balaklava of the 25th ultimo, given in the papers
which have just arrived from England, you observe
"that from some misconception of the instruction to
advance, the Lieutenant-General considered that he

was bound to attack at all hazards, and he accordingly ordered Lord Cardigan to move forward with the light brigade." Surely, my Lord, this is a grave charge, and an imputation reflecting seriously upon my professional character. I cannot remain silent; it is, I feel, incumbent on me to state those facts which I cannot doubt must clear me from what I respectfully submit is altogether unmerited.

The cavalry was formed to support an intended movement of the infantry, when Captain Nolan, the aide-de-camp of the Quartermaster-General, came up to me at speed and placed in my hand this instruction:

> (Copy)
> "Lord Raglan wishes the cavalry to advance
> rapidly to the front to follow the enemy, and
> try to prevent the enemy carrying away the
> guns. Troop of horse artillery may accompany.
> French cavalry is on your left."
> "Immediate"
> (signed)
> "R. Airey"
> Quartermaster-General

After carefully reading the order, I hesitated and urged the uselessness of such an attack, and the dangers attending it. The aide-de-camp, in a most authoritative tone, stated that they were Lord Raglan's orders, that the cavalry should attack immediately. I asked where, and to do what, as neither enemy nor

guns were within sight? He replied in the most disrespectful but significant manner, pointing to the
further end of the valley, "There, my Lord, is your
enemy; there are your guns."

So distinct in my opinion was your written
instruction, and so positive and urgent were the
orders delivered by the aide-de-camp, that I felt it was
imperative on me to obey; and I informed Lord
Cardigan that he was to advance; and to the objec-
tions he made, in which I entirely agreed, I replied
that the orders were from your Lordship.

Having decided, against my conviction, to make
the movement, I did all in my power to render it as
little perilous as possible. I formed the light brigade in
two lines, and led to its support two regiments of
heavy cavalry, the Scots Greys and the Royal
Dragoons, only halting them when they had reached
the point from which they could protect the retreat
of the light cavalry, in the event of their being pursued by the enemy, and when having lost many
officers and men from the batteries and fort, any further advances would have exposed them to
destruction. My Lord, I considered at the time—I am
still of the same opinion—that I followed the only
course open to me. As a lieutenant-general, doubtless
I have discretionary power; but to take upon myself to
disobey an order written by my Commander-in-
Chief, within a few minutes of the delivery, and given
from an elevated position, commanding an entire
view of all the batteries and the position of the
enemy, would have been nothing less than direct

disobedience of orders, without any other reason than I preferred my own opinion to that of my general; and in this instance must have exposed me and the cavalry to aspersions, against which it might have been difficult to defend ourselves.

It should be remembered that the aide-de-camp, well informed of the instructions of his general, and the object he had in view, after first insisting on an immediate charge, then placed himself in front of one of the leading squadrons, when he fell the first victim.

I did not dare to disobey your Lordship, and it is the opinion of every officer of rank in this army, to whom I have shown the written order, that it was not possible for me to do so.

I hope, my Lord, that I have stated the facts temperately, and in a becoming and respectful manner, as it has been my wish to do.

I am confident that it will be your desire to do me justice; I will only ask that your Lordship should kindly give the same publicity to this letter as has been given to your report, for I am sensitively anxious to satisfy my Sovereign, my military superiors, and the public, that I have not on this unhappy occasion shown myself undeserving of their confidence, or unfitting the command which I hold.

I have etc.

(signed)

Lucan

Lieutenant-General Commanding Cavalry Division

Duke of Newcastle to Field Marshal Lord Raglan

War Department 27th January 1855

My Lord,

I have to acknowledge your Lordship's despatch, dated 16th December, enclosing the copy of a letter addressed to you by Lieutenant-General the Earl of Lucan and submitting to me observations on its contents.

Upon the receipt of that despatch I felt that the public service and the general discipline of the army would be greatly prejudiced by any misunderstanding between your Lordship, as the general commanding Her Majesty's forces in the field, and the Lieutenant-General commanding the division of cavalry; but desiring to be fortified, in all matters of this nature, by the opinions of the General Commanding-in-Chief, I submitted, without delay, your Lordship's despatch and the letter of the Earl of Lucan, for the considera-tion of General the Viscount Hardinge.

I have now the honour of enclosing, for your Lordship's guidance, an extract from the reply which I have this day received from Lord Hardinge, and which has been submitted to and approved by the Queen.

I have, therefore, to instruct your Lordship to communicate this decision to the Earl of Lucan, and to inform his Lordship that he should resign the com-mand of the cavalry and return to England.

In performing this painful duty, I purposely abstain from any comments upon the correspondence submitted to me; but I must observe that, apart from any consideration of the merits of the question raised by Lord Lucan, the position in which he has now placed himself towards your Lordship renders his withdrawal from the army under your command in all respects advisable.

I have etc.

(signed)

Newcastle

Extract of a letter from Viscount Hardinge to His Grace the Duke of Newcastle dated Horse Guards 26th January 1855

It is to be regretted that the Lieutenant-General, acting upon a misconception of a written order, did not show the order to Lord Cardigan; and that, influenced by the authoritative tone and disrespectful manner of the aide-de-camp, did not decide upon his own judgment, supported by the concurrence of his major-general, that the charge ought not to be made.

Lord Lucan, in his letter of the 30th November, objects to the terms used by Lord Raglan, in his public despatch, that his orders for the light brigade to charge were given under a misconception of the written order etc. He declines to withdraw that letter, and adheres to the construction he has put upon the order, that it compelled him to direct a charge.

The papers having been referred by your Grace to me, I concur with Lord Raglan, that the terms he used in his despatch were appropriate; and as a good understanding between the Field-Marshal commanding the forces in the field, and the Lieutenant-General commanding the cavalry division, are conditions essentially necessary for advantageously carrying on the public service, I recommend that Lieutenant-General Lord Lucan should be recalled; and if your Grace and Her Majesty's Government concur in this view, I will submit my recommendation to Her Majesty and take Her Majesty's pleasure on the subject.

PART 2

*Evidence given to Parliamentary Commissioners
concerning the conditions for the care of the sick both
en route to and at
the Crimea and subsequently on board the hospital ships
bound for Scutari.*

Shipping routes in the Black Sea during the Crimean War

Battle of the Alma.........20th September, 1854
Battle of Balaklava.........25th October, 1854
Battle of Inkerman.........5th November, 1854

Sea of Azov

Str. of Kerch

CRIMEA

Eupatoria

R. Alma
Inkerman
Sebastopol
Balaklava

B L A C K   S E A

Invasion force of 50,000
land on 14th Sept, 1854

Allied force sails into
Black Sea to Varna

Bosphorous

Varna

Sea of
Marmora

Constantinople

Scutari (Florence Nightingale's hospital)

0   100   200   300 miles

N

In January 1855, Mr Alexander, the staff surgeon of the Light Cavalry, reported on his experience of the medical conditions in which he had been working since arriving in the East.

Camp, Heights, Sebastopol, January 15th, 1855

GENTLEMEN,

Having arrived at Varna, the Light Division (of which I was then in medical charge) was encamped at a short distance from the town. On being ordered on to Aladyn, it was with the greatest difficulty that the smallest allowance of transport was granted by the military authorities. No medicine chests, reserve supplies of medicines, or comforts were allowed to be carried, not even a small supply of medicine for the staff, &c. We were encamped at Aladyn for some time; and hearing that we were likely to move forward, I endeavoured to obtain a second supply of medicines and comforts to accompany us, and eventually wrote a letter to General Airey, then commanding the division in the field, stating how we were circumstanced, and what misery and wretchedness would ensue unless a supply of the above stores were allowed to accompany the Division.

He forwarded my letter to General Brown, who referred the same, with some remarks, to the Principal Medical Officer; but as I had also written to him, urging that a supply should be sent out to accompany us, he, the Principal Medical Officer, took my view of the case, and wrote to General Brown requesting that a supply should be permitted to join the Division and accompany it, which was eventually done.

A medicine chest was also got, after great difficulty, for the staff, &c.; at the same time I was ordered, on our moving forward, to hand the same over to those that relieved us, and if not relieved, it was to be returned to Varna. Surely, if requisite at Aladyn, it was equally, if not more so, when further removed to head-quarters.

We moved to Devna, and had not been long there before cholera, in its most malignant form, broke out among the troops, and luckily the small supply of medicines and comforts we then had, were of some use in alleviating the distress of the sufferers. We proceeded to Monastir, where cholera continued to rage among us while we remained there; and there it was, although thirty miles or so distant from the headquarters at Varna, it was with much difficulty that small supplies of the most necessary medicines and comforts could be obtained; so much so, that I authorised the medical officers to purchase whatever they could, and was requisite for their sick, &c., that could not be obtained from the limited stores of the Division, and that I myself would be responsible for the payment of the same, should the Government refuse to pay the amount. The requisitions were so tardily complied with, that, during the height of cholera, one dated 5th August, sent off early on the morning of the 6th, and approved by the Principal Medical Officer on the 7th, still the medicines did not reach Monastir until 4 P.M. on the 18th, and the reason given by the Principal Medical Officer, "the medicines have been ready for days, but as it was not an araba★ road, we had no means of sending it out." Again, the medical comforts were issued so liberally, that at one time three pounds of arrowroot was sent for the whole Division; at another, I was informed "that the demand for essence of beef amounts to almost the whole of the supply originally sent from England."

We moved from Monastir to Varna, and when within a day's march or so of the latter, I heard we

---

★ A heavy screened wagon used by the Tartars and others.

were intended for the Crimea. I rode into Varna next morning, and as our supplies of medicines and comforts had been doled out to us in such small quantities, I trusted as we were certainly going into an enemy's country, and consequently to be engaged in certain warfare, and as they had been nearly expended, I fully expected that ample supplies both of medicines and comforts would have been ready prepared for each Division. On seeing the Principal Medical Officer, and telling him the exhausted state of our medicines and comforts, and that I trusted a good supply was ready for the Division to take with them, I was coolly told, "It was my business, not his."

I begged to differ from him, and said, I was not even aware that I was going to the Crimea, &c. &c.; he then told me I might order the surgeons to send in their panniers. I did so, and those of the First Brigade got in some measure replenished; not so, however, the Second Brigade, as they being behind had not time.

We embarked on the 30th August, and having gone on board the "Emperor" steamship, I found about 500 men and officers of the 7th Fusiliers, with two assistant surgeons, but without one grain of medicine. I desired one of them to go on shore at once and obtain a supply; he succeeded in getting a small medicine chest, which he brought on board with him. Unfortunately cholera broke out on board on the passage to the Crimea, and having embarked on the 30th August, and disembarked on the 14th September, with such a disease prevailing, it may easily be imagined that the pannier supply was all but expended.

My Division marched the same day they landed about six miles into the country. Cholera still continued amongst us, and several fatal cases occurred in the 88th Regiment. I went in daily to the landing-place to see the Principal Medical Officer. I, however, did not succeed in seeing him until the 17th; he was then on the beach. On my telling him how we were situated as regarded medicines, comforts, &c., I was informed that "I was making difficulties."

I replied "Those of the Light Division never make difficulties." He then said, "Make a requisition." Dr. Pine, who was present, asked him "If one was made could the same be complied with?" when it was elicited that some supplies were on board some ship, but where she was, was quite another thing. We got nothing of course.

We marched on the 19th, and fought the battle of Alma. On the 20th, when the Light Division had about 1,000 killed and wounded, there were no ambulances &c. &c., or lights (save the personal property of the officers)—nearly all the operations requiring to be performed on the ground. I, myself, operated the whole of the first day on the poor fellows on the ground, and had performed many on the second (two of them being hip joint cases), until an old door was discovered, of which we made a table, and of course performed all my other operations (including another hip joint case on a Russian) on the same. Had it not been for the French and the navy,

Heaven only knows how we could have had our wounded moved to the shipping. On the first day of the battle, several hundreds of the Light Division had the necessary operations performed, and their wounds dressed, &c.

A marquee and some tents were pitched, and waterdecks, waterproof bed-covers, and blankets were issued to all, and tea, chocolate, wine, brandy, &c., were distributed to all the sufferers requiring the same. The chocolate, with some blankets, sugar, and the marquees, were supplied from the head-quarters stores. We marched on the 23rd, and reached Balaklava, and eventually came hither.

Being so close to Balaklava, only about seven miles distant, whence steamers were continually plying between it and Scutari, I was in hope that supplies of medicines, comforts, beds, bedding, tents, marquees, &c., would have been liberally issued. But, alas! such was not destined to take place. We have been much worse off here for medicines, comforts, &c., than we were in Bulgaria; in proof of which, with a sick list of 636, of cholera, dysentery, diarrhœa, fevers, &c., on the 1st December four ounces of pulv. opii, and the same of calomel were issued for the Division, which was about three doses of one grain of each of these two medicines to each patient: of other most important medicines none could be supplied; others were much curtailed. Again, on the 13th December, one ounce of pulv. opii and four ounces of blue pill were sent to the Division, consisting of eight and a half battalions, besides marines and artillery, the sick list being 619, of cholera, dysentery, diarrhoea, fevers, &c.

About the same period, although the troops were on sufficient rations, few or no medical comforts could be had, there being at the time neither sago nor arrowroot when applied for, &c. Now, I must acknowledge, with the ample supplies sent out by the Director-General for any contingency, and command of the Constantinople market, I cannot conceive why anything tending to the comfort of the sick and wounded was not always at hand when required, both in Bulgaria as well as here in the Crimea, more particularly as we had command of the sea, and steamers continually plying, both when we were in Bulgaria, between Scutari and Varna, and now between the former and Balaklava.

The misery and wretchedness the troops have suffered here, but more particularly the sick, are scarcely credible, and require to be seen to be believed—poor sick wretches lying on the ground, with some miserable blankets, in tents that let in rain as if they were sieves, and with no fuel save the miserable brushwood and roots that could be gathered for cooking, &c. Marquees have now, however, been got for all the regiments, and some bedsteads of Clarke's, Smith's, &c., have been obtained; but the latter, unfortunately, are without feet, and the cross parts for keeping them stretched. Some buffalo robes have also been obtained. Trestle beds and fuel have been issued latterly, but the same must be brought up from Balaklava, which is no easy matter with the present transport; still, what with the above, waterdecks, extra blankets, tarpaulins, as well as a better supply of medicines and comforts, the patients are somewhat more comfortable, but still treatment is of little use in tents or marquees, although stoves are placed in them, with more than a foot of snow on the ground during a Crimean winter. Great misery has also been caused from the want of transport for the sick, our ambulances having been latterly quite useless, so that we have been nearly entirely indebted to French ambulance mule corps for the removal of our sick, with the exception once of our sick being sent down on cavalry horses, which thinned the marquees, &c., but did not remove those cases that required it most, they being unable to sit on horseback.

From the above statement of facts I think the Board will perceive that much blame is due somewhere for all the wretchedness and misery that has taken place during the present campaign, and which, in my opinion, could have been so easily prevented, and I sincerely hope they will be the means of placing the blame on the proper persons, and preventing similar scenes of wretchedness and misery in the ensuing campaign.

It is due to the medical officers of the Division, as well as those in charge of medicines and purveyors' stores, to state, that no men could have worked harder, or performed more zealously their arduous and onerous duties, both in Bulgaria during the ravages of cholera, as well as in the Crimea, and that none of them have spared either trouble or inconvenience in doing all they could to obtain whatever would tend to the comforts of their sick, &c., &c.

I may add in conclusion, that several divisions have applied to me for medicines and comforts—one for one bottle of wine, half pound of arrowroot, and one pound of sago when at Monastir, and they had to come about two miles for the same. Again, I received an express from a first-class staff surgeon in charge of a cavalry brigade, requesting me to send him some medicines, as "he was completely run out of every-thing," and his men were dying from cholera. One of the surgeons of the Light Division called upon me one afternoon, and told me had come from visiting a General Officer of another Division (a personal friend of his), who was severely wounded, and as he had nothing, he intended sending him some essence of beef, and hoped that I did not consider that he was wrong in doing so. Others have also applied to the Light Division for extras, &c., but the above will show how some other Divisions were provided, &c., &c., and the above facts speak for themselves.

I have, &c.,

(Signed)

T. ALEXANDER,

Staff Surgeon, 1st Class in Medical Charge, Light Division.

Carriage of the sick and necessary medical supplies during army operations before Sebastopol.

No vehicles of any kind were appropriated for the carriage of the men who were compelled to fall out from sickness during the march from Kalamita Bay to Balaklava. The arabas used for carrying commissariat stores and artillery waggons appear to have been the only conveyances to which the men, under such circumstances, were able to resort; but this accommodation was necessarily limited and precarious.

The marches in the Crimea were not long, but cholera existed in the army; and we have reason to fear that men were lost in consequence of the want of means for carrying those who fell ill on the march. Lieut.-Colonel Egerton mentioned to us, on the occasion of our visiting the field hospital of the 77th Regiment, on the 9th of January, that a man of that regiment having been taken sick on the march was placed on the side of the road along which the commissariat arabas and artillery waggons were expected to pass, in the hope that he would be taken up by them, but that he had never been heard of afterwards.

After the battle of the Alma, the wounded were carried to the shore, partly on stretchers by bandsmen, sailors and others, partly in arabas, or waggons of the country, and partly by the mules of the French ambulance.

The want of the ambulance waggons was much felt on this occasion, and we believe that great delay in collecting the wounded, and dressing their wounds, was the consequence. The action on the Alma was fought on the 20th September, and, according to Dr. Hall, it was not until the evening of the 22nd that all the wounded were dressed and sent on board ship.

The ambulance waggons, from the time of their arrival in the Crimea early in October, until about the middle of November, appear to have been of much service, both in carrying the sick and wounded from the camp to Balaklava, and also in removing the wounded from the front to the rear at the battle of

Inkerman. When the wet weather set in, however, and the roads, or rather tracks, between the camp and Balaklava, became wet and broken up, the waggons were found less and less available, and the use of them was finally abandoned early in January. They are considered by Dr. Hall, and many other officers, as too heavy; and this opinion appears to us to be well founded.

Their number also, two to each division, was insufficient for the removal of the large number of sick brought down from the camp to Balaklava since the end of November.

Artillery waggons were called in aid for this purpose, and artillery horses were harnessed as leaders to the ambulance waggons, when the state of the roads or of the ambulance horses rendered the latter unable to draw their load. The valuable assistance of the mules belonging to the French ambulance was also obtained, and as many as 500 of these animals, equipped each with a pair of seats, or a pair of litters hanging on either side of the pack saddle, have been employed on a single day in carrying our sick from the heights before Sebastopol to Balaklava. Our own cavalry horses have been lately employed in bringing down such of the patients as could ride; but this means of transport is unsuitable for the sick, and is wholly unavailable, except for the least severe cases of illness or injury.

The ambulance corps does not appear to have answered the expectations which were originally entertained respecting it. "From their habits and age," says Dr. Hall, speaking of these men, "they are quite unfitted for their situation. They could not drive. There were no smiths, farriers, or wheel-wrights with them, so that the most trifling damage rendered the carriages useless." We found that this opinion was shared by many other persons.

The animals belonging to them have for the most part died; and at present, we believe, the corps is of no service whatever.

For the carriage of medicines, surgical appliances, and medical comforts, one *bât poney* [packhorse] was allotted to each regiment. The articles in question were packed in two small panniers. No provision was made for the carriage of the A and B canteens—the two boxes in which culinary and other articles of the regimental hospital furniture are contained. These were not carried on the march to Balaklava; but, under ordinary circumstances, a second *bât poney* is allotted for their carriage.

The suggestions which we would beg to make with respect to this branch of the subject are:—

1 That every regiment should be provided with one or two light vehicles, for the carriage of the sick, wounded, and fatigued soldiers on the march. Such vehicles as those recommended by Dr. Hall, resembling the Bianconi Irish jaunting car, would probably be found suitable for this purpose.

2 That our ambulance corps should be formed of carefully selected men in the prime of life, and younger than those who now constitute that body;

that there should be in their ranks wheelwrights, farriers, harness-makers, and other artisans, so that any injuries to the vehicles, harness, and equipments of the animals employed should always be easily repaired; and that the men should also undergo some training as hospital orderlies.

3 That the ambulance waggons should, if practicable, be made of a lighter construction than those now in use.

4 That a body of mules, equipped like the mules of the French ambulance, should be formed, as an auxiliary to the ambulance waggons. The animals should be of the largest and most powerful kind. As experience has proved, they would be found of essential service in carrying sick and slightly wounded men, where ambulance waggons, from the want of roads, or the badness of them, would be of no avail.

5 That more ample means than those hitherto allowed should be supplied for the transport of hospital stores, furniture, medicines, medical comforts, surgical instruments and appliances, and culinary apparatus. We think that the several articles now packed in the regimental panniers, and in the A and B canteens, might be more easily carried in a small two-wheeled cart resembling that taken from the Russians by the artillery, which we examined at Balaklava.

6 Larger vehicles, like the French four-wheeled "caissons", might be advantageously employed in carrying the reserve stores of medicines and medical comforts of the division.

⊶⊷

Hospital accommodation in the field.

With respect to the hospital accommodation, medical attendance, supply of medicines and medical comforts in the field, we examined Dr. Hall, and Mr. Jenner, the purveyor at Balaklava; and in order to collect in the shortest time as large a mass of information as possible on the same subject, we addressed to the surgeons of regiments a series of written questions, copies of which were also forwarded to the commanding officers of regiments, with the request that they would favour us with any information in their possession on the subject referred to in our queries.

The hospital accommodation allowed to each regiment upon the invasion of the Crimea was one bell tent. A few marquees were put on board the "John Masterman", which carried the purveyors' and apothecaries' reserve stores of the expedition. Three of these were landed on the 18th of September, but only two of them were put up on the day of the battle of the Alma. The men who were wounded in that engagement were, according to Dr. Hall, collected in some houses in a vineyard, or placed in rows in a farmyard littered with hay. The supply of medicines and surgical appliances, exclusive of those carried in the regimental panniers, and medical comforts landed in Kalamita Bay, and taken with the army on its march, have been furnished to us by Dr. Hall.

We believe that this supply was found sufficient at the battle of the Alma, with the exception of long thigh splints, and brandy. Complaints have been made to us by two surgeons, that they could not get long splints on that day; and it appears from the evidence of Mr. Jenner, the purveyor, that he did not fully comply with the demands made upon him for brandy.

By an oversight, no candles were included among the stores brought to the Crimea. Lamps and wicks were brought, but not oil. These omissions were not supplied until after possession had been taken of Balaklava, and the purveyor had an opportunity of purchasing candles and oil from the shipping and the dealers in the town.

It appears to us, that the hospital accommodation in the field for the sick and wounded has been very inadequate.

The nature of this accommodation was, in our opinion, wholly unsuitable for the treatment of the sick and wounded in winter. Even the most comfortable marquee is not free from objection for such a purpose; but bell-tents, as well from the materials of which they are made as from their shape and size, are peculiarly ill adapted for hospital purposes. They are not always wind or water-tight, and they do not admit of more than three or four stretchers or any other form of bedstead being used in them.

The quantity as well as the quality of hospital accommodation was in our opinion insufficient. In numerous instances we found that many of the sick were treated in their own tents, for want of room in the hospital tents or marquees of their regiments. Although all the men who were on the sick list did not necessarily require admission into hospital, we believe that a considerable number of those described as attending hospital were not admitted into it simply because there was no room for them.

In the 88th Regiment, of the 120 men on the sick list on the day of our visit, 24 or 25 alone were in hospital, but more than double that number, we were assured by the surgeon, needed hospital accommodation. On the day of our visit to the field hospital of the Sappers and Miners, the surgeon in charge informed us that he had 14 patients whom he was desirous of getting into the hospital marquee, but that he was unable to do so from want of room.

We found a general want of bedsteads, stretchers, and every other means of raising the men above the ground. Even of the small supply of Smith's and Clarke's stretchers at the disposal of the surgeons only a portion was used, owing partly to the insufficient number of marquees and tents available for hospital purposes, and partly to the incompleteness of the stretchers, many of which were without legs and without the transverse bars which keep them stretched.

With few exceptions, the men were without mattresses or palliasses. They lay, in general, on a blanket stretched over water-decks or rush mats. In one case, underwood was placed under them. In another, the surgeon had spread white marl over the ground. In the tents of the 5th Dragoon Guards the patients had hay under them. We saw no bolsters or pillows; the patient's knapsack ordinarily served for this purpose. The supply of blankets was in some cases sufficient; but the men were often limited to their field allowance. This was, in some cases, a single blanket, for although a second had been generally distributed towards the middle of December, as we were informed, this distribution had not been universal. We did not see sheets in the camp.

Few of the marquees or tents were supplied with stoves, or any other means whatever of heating.

The supply of hospital utensils, also, appears to us to have been far too limited, when regard is paid to the number of sick, and the prevalent complaints— diarrhœa and dysentery. Mr. Jenner informed us that he had not, on the day when we examined him (January 10th), a single urinal, bed-pan, or close-stool complete. He said that he had plenty of frames, but that the pans had not reached him. He also said that he had often been obliged to refuse requisitions for such things to regiments, especially recently. We found, however, in his store plenty of frames and metal vessels, which, though not destined for this purpose, answered for completing the article in question.

Hospital clothing was not used in the Crimea. Six hundred hospital dresses were brought into the country; but neither those dresses, nor flannel waistcoats, nor any articles of hospital clothing, were ever issued, as no requisitions were made for them either from the regiments or from the hospital at Balaklava. We found the men in the field hospitals lying in their uniforms and great coats. The only portion of their dress of which they appeared to be divested was their boots.

In the hospitals in the camp the men appeared in general supplied with warm under clothing; but their coatees, trowsers, and great coats seemed, in many cases, much worn. In the hospitals of the heavy cavalry, which we visited some days later, we found the patients supplied with pea coats, buffalo robes, sheepskins, and waterproof coats.

With respect to the medical attendance in the field, we think that it has been sufficient, notwithstanding that sickness, and detachment on other duty, have thinned the ranks of the regimental surgeons. The only case in which we thought the supply insufficient was in that of the Sappers and Miners, numbering altogether about 300 men, and having on the day of our visit 16 men in hospital, besides 54 off duty. The only medical officer attached to this body was a young staff assistant surgeon, the eighth medical man, according to the hospital sergeant, who had been in charge of it since the army left England.

From Lieutenant-Colonel Egerton, of the 77th, who accompanied us through his hospital marquee and tents, we learnt that the surgeon of his regiment was ill at the time of our visit, that the first assistant surgeon was in medical charge of the artillerymen of a battery, that the second had been sent in charge of sick to Scutari, and that upon the third fell the entire attendance of the sick of the regiment. The 44th Regiment was equally unfortunate in this respect. But this inconvenience was quite temporary, and, with the single exception above mentioned, of the Sappers and Miners, we have no reason whatever to doubt the sufficiency of the supply of regimental medical officers.

The orderlies and other hospital attendants were also, in point of numbers, sufficient; but we are informed that in some instances many of these men did not receive the pay of orderlies, but were employed as fatigue men. With respect to their quali- fications for their office, we reserve our remarks to a later portion of our Report.

The means of cooking were deficient. Fuel was very scarce, and consisted either of charcoal brought up from Balaklava, or of the roots of trees dug up chiefly at the extreme right of the camp, where the battle of Inkerman was fought. The supply of the most necessary culinary utensils was everywhere scanty, although Mr. Jenner assured us that he had never been without them in store. The cooking was everywhere performed in the open air.

When it could be procured, fresh meat was, according to Dr. Hall, given to the sick; but, according to the same authority, they had not had any for weeks. In that case, preserved meat was issued by the purveyor; but, according to the evidence of Dr. Alexander and some of the regimental surgeons, the sick have been frequently left upon salt rations.

The supply of medicines and medical comforts appears to have been in some important particulars very insufficient. Upon this point we have the almost unanimous testimony of regimental surgeons, surgeons of divisions, and the Principal Medical Officer of the British Army in the East. We have also the evidence of Mr. Kersey and Mr. Jenner, the dispenser and the purveyor at Balaklava, from whose stores the camp is supplied. The former gentleman informed us that his first stock of the preparations of opium and astringents was exhausted by the middle of October. It would appear that this want continued to be felt, more or less severely, from the period mentioned by Mr. Kersey, down to the middle of January. From copies which we obtained of requisitions which the apothecary was unable to comply with, between 1st and 9th of January, it appears that the want still existed down to the latter date; but as we saw in his office, a few days later, a box containing 50 lbs. of crude opium, then just arrived from Constantinople, we hope and believe that the army is at the present moment fully supplied with the usual preparations of that drug.

The medicines of which the want was chiefly felt were the different preparations of opium, except morphine, of which, it appears from Dr. Hall's evidence, there was always a supply. The articles of medical comforts which were deficient were chiefly sago, arrowroot, ground rice, essence of beef, preserved meat, and brandy. The purveyor informed us that he had often been obliged to buy candles, tea, and other articles from the settlers and the shipping.

We attempted to form some estimate of the extent of these deficiencies by questioning the surgeons of the regiments. According to the ordinary practice, when a regimental surgeon is in want of medicines and medical comforts, he applies to the principal medical officer of his division for a supply. This officer, if he approves of the requisition, countersigns it, and the required articles are issued by the apothecary or the purveyor's clerk in charge of the stores attached to the division. When the stock of medicines and medical comforts in these stores began to fail, the regimental surgeons endeavoured to get their wants supplied by the apothecary and purveyor at Balaklava, where the principal stores in the Crimea are kept. This practice entailed upon these latter gentlemen a great addition to their ordinary labours, and upon the surgeons the inconvenience of sending several miles for their supplies. This inconvenience became gradually aggravated in proportion as it became frequent, and its frequency became more and more necessary as the quantities that were dealt out at a time to them, in answer to their requisitions, became smaller. The practice, under such circumstances, of requiring the counter-signature of the medical officer in charge of divisions, operated very vexatiously.

We obtained the required information from a few surgeons only, but from their returns a fair estimate may probably be formed of the deficiencies under consideration. With the same object, we subsequently requested the medical officers in charge of divisions to favour us with returns of the requisition which they had made for the replenishment of their stores, and the extent to which those requisitions had been complied with. Such returns we obtained from Dr. Alexander and Dr. Linton, the medical officers in charge of the Light and 1st Divisions.

We have only to observe respecting these several documents, that while the answers to the demands show the poverty of the stores on which the demands were made, the demands themselves are by no means to be understood as exhibiting the extent of the wants experienced; for we ascertained that when it became known that the supplies were short, the requisitions were framed with reference, not to the just wants of the stores to be replenished, but to the probable or ascertained state of those on which the demands were made. The extreme scarcity of powdered opium in December may be judged of from the statement in Dr. Alexander's communication, that on the 1st of that month four ounces of the medicine in question was the quantity issued to the Light

Division, which then had a sick list of 636 patients suffering from cholera, dysentery, diarrhœa, and fever, while on the 13th only one ounce was issued to the same division, which then had 619 sick.

We have to add, that we found the patients in the field hospitals generally in a very filthy condition. The want of bedsteads, already noticed, partially accounts for this, for it was impossible that the men should, under such circumstances, escape from the mud. But besides the dirt arising from this cause, they had evidently been long unwashed and uncombed. The loss of their kits, which had been made so frequently the subject of complaint to us at Scutari, appears one of the chief causes of the vermin which was, if not general, at all events not uncommon among them. This loss arose principally from their having, in obedience to orders to that effect, left their packs on board the vessels which transported them to the Crimea, and from their having been unable to recover them afterwards.

As we are enjoined by the terms of our Commission to offer suggestions for the correction of existing deficiencies, it was necessary that we should inquire into the causes of the several wants above mentioned.

From the evidence of Dr. Hall, Dr. Anderson, Messrs. Jenner, Kersey, and Fernandes, it would seem that the want of medicines, medical comforts, and several articles of hospital furniture was attributable partly to tardy and imperfect compliance with orders and requisitions on Scutari, and partly to the difficulty of ascertaining on board what vessels stores were laden, and of landing those stores when such information was obtained. The want of huts, marquees, stores, and bedsteads, of which Mr. Jenner says he always had a supply, was generally imputed to the want of means of transporting such articles from Balaklava to the camp. The imperfect state in which we found Smith's and Clarke's stretchers in the camp was stated by Dr. Hall to have been owing to the fact that different portions of them were shipped on board different vessels. The frames, it would seem, arrived at Balaklava by the "Jura" last November, while the legs were sent by the "Robert Lowe", which did not reach that harbour until the end of December.

To test the accuracy of the first statement, it would have been necessary to enter upon an inquiry into the conduct of individuals, and this we thought it was not competent for us to do. We confine ourselves, therefore, to the statement, that the supply of medicines and medical comforts was in point of fact greatly deficient in the Crimea, without expressing any opinion as to the causes of that deficiency. With respect to the alleged want of means of transport, any formal inquiry was superfluous, as we personally witnessed, day after day, during our three weeks' stay in the Crimea, the transport of fuel, clothing, and food from Balaklava to the camp by fatigue parties. We were informed, besides, by several officers, that they had obtained orders for huts and marquees, but that they had not got these up to the camp, as they were required to transport them, and they did not possess sufficient means for that purpose.

We learnt that the issue to regiments of huts and marquees and other articles was made only upon requisition. We think that the consequence of this practice may be observed in the hospital accommodation. The condition of the sick varies in every regiment, and it varies in great measure with the energy and zeal of the commanding and medical officers, and with the means of transport at their disposal. We think that the state of the men should not be left dependent on such circumstances.

From the evidence of Dr. Hall and Dr. Anderson, it appears that the notice of the intended removal of sick from the camp which is given to the medical officers has sometimes been very brief. As this removal has been frequently dependent on the assistance of the French ambulance corps, it may not have been always possible to give more time for preparation than that which has been allowed; but the want of timely notification has occasionally caused great hurry and confusion, both in despatching the men from the camp and in preparing for their embarkation at Balaklava.

The suggestions which we would beg to offer with reference to this branch of the subject are:—

1 That the sick should, with the exception only of such slight cases as appear to need but a few days' hospital attendance, be removed with all practicable despatch from the field to the rear. Under the most

favourable circumstances it is extremely difficult to treat successfully in the field any but very slight cases; and we think that this is especially difficult under canvas, in winter, with cases of diarrhœa, dysentery, scurvy, and frost-bite—the prevalent affections which we found in the camp.

2 That the sick should not be removed without a reasonable notice having been first given to the medical officer whose duty it is to provide for their wants upon their arrival at their immediate destination.

3 That every regiment should always be supplied at once with its due allowance of hospital accommodation and furniture, without requisition.

4 That a store of medicines and medical comforts sufficient for the probable wants of the army for three months, should always be kept at head quarters, or some other place easily accessible to the various divisions of the army.

5 That the store of medicines and medical comforts kept with the regiment should always be sufficient for at least a fortnight's probable consumption.

6 That these stores should be replenished periodically from the principal store without requisition.

7 That when the regimental stores fail before their periodical replenishment, the requisition of the regimental surgeon should be complied with, without needing the approval of the medical officer of the division; and, to prevent fraud, that the whole of the requisition should be in the handwriting of the surgeon.

8 That the men should be daily inspected on their return from duty, whether in the trenches or on picket or elsewhere, by one of the medical officers of the regiment. We attach peculiar importance to this step in winter, when men are exposed to frost-bite—an injury of which they frequently are not conscious until it has assumed a grave character.

9 With a view of obtaining a good class of hospital attendants for the service, we shall have to offer some suggestions when we come to the hospitals at Scutari. In the event of those suggestions not meeting with your Grace's approval, we would recommend, in this place, that the rank, pay, and pension of the hospital sergeant should be equal to that of the highest non-commissioned regimental officer, and that the pay of hospital orderlies should be raised to such an amount as would attract ser-viceable men to the situation.

When the sick and wounded are carried from the camp to Balaklava, they are either admitted into the hospital in that place, or they are embarked on board vessels for Scutari.

Concerning the medical conditions on board ships destined for Scutari.

The sick and wounded who are destined for Scutari are at once taken to the wharf, where a medical officer is in attendance to see to their embarkation, and to afford medical assistance when necessary. The men are embarked in boats, under the orders of a naval officer, and put on board the vessels which have been prepared for their reception.

This duty was at first entrusted altogether to the principal medical officer at Balaklava. On one occasion, we learn, boats were not ready for the reception of the sick. This arose, according to Dr. Tice, who was then Principal Medical Officer at Balaklava, in consequence of his not having received the verbal notice which had been sent to him by another medical officer of the intended arrival of patients. Except in this instance, we did not hear of any delay having arisen, beyond that incidental to the necessarily slow process of embarking a large number of helpless men in a limited number of open boats, and transhipping them to larger vessels. We think, however, with Dr. Anderson, that the practice of sending down to the harbour from 600 to 1,200 men together for embarkation, has endangered the lives of many, in wet weather, from the long exposure on the beach to which they were subjected. They ought to be sent in much smaller detachments, so that the whole number in each detachment might be taken on board at once.

Subsequently to the occasion referred to, a General Order directed that an officer of the Quartermaster General's department should accompany the men from the camp to the harbour, with a view of seeing to their proper embarkation. A medical officer is sent on board before the sick embark, in order to see to their proper arrangement and accommodation.

There is the question of whether sufficient space was allotted to the sick and wounded soldiers on board the vessels in which they were transported. Although we are, however, from the want of the necessary data, unable to pronounce a confident opinion upon this point with respect to every ship, there are many on the above list as to which we do not hesitate to express our conviction that they were much overcrowded. Judging from the size of the "Kangaroo," and from the scanty information which we obtained from the junior medical officer on board—the senior being dead—we do not think that she was large enough to carry 400 sick men, besides 24 officers, suffering from cholera. We cannot doubt, also, that the "Andes" and "Colombo," on their first voyage, and the "Orient" and the "Caduceus," were greatly overcrowded. Having come from Balaklava to this place in the "Cleopatra" on her voyage in January, we think that she had at least 40 men too many on board on that occasion, and, consequently, that she was much overcrowded on her former voyage also. With respect to the vessels which have been represented to us by the medical officers in charge of them as too crowded, although we are not in a position to confirm their opinion with confidence, we have no reason to doubt the truth of their representations. We think, further, that whenever the men have been in fact limited to the space mentioned by Dr. Anderson as that which is allowed by the Board of Inspection at Balaklava in its calculation of the number of patients which a vessel can properly carry, they have been overcrowded; and if that rule has been strictly observed by the Board ever since its formation on the 12th December, we must declare that every vessel which brought down sick and wounded men from

Table of deaths on board ships travelling from the Crimea to the Bosphorous.

Name of vessel	No. of deaths
Kangaroo	?
Dunbar	22
Cambria	–
Vulcan	18
Andes	15
Colombo	30
Arthur the Great	24
Orient	33
Caduceus	114
Couries	16
Cornwall	6
Negotiator	6
Lady McNaughton	3
Australian	8
Cumbrian	–
Echunga	7
Palmerston	11
Tynemouth	15
Shooting Star	20
Colombo	4
Sidney	2
Talavera	10
Arabia	4
Mauritius	12
Andes	8
Edendale	38
Medway	23
Trent	2
Avon	52

Table of deaths cont'd

Sovereign	–
Gertrude	39
Blundell	6
Candia	–
Cleopatra	31
Ripon	14
Golden Fleece	15
Timandra	31
Victoria	20
Brandon	5
Gomelza	11
Ottawa	13
Joseph Shepherd	12
Australian	2
Harbinger	7
Jason	12
Belgravia	38
Thames	–
Colombo	27
St. Hilda	20
Niagara	11
Nubia	2
Brandon	8
Cleopatra	17?
Shooting Star	47
Pedestrian	19
Golden Fleece	11
Melbourne	2
Total	923

the Crimea to Scutari subsequently to that date was overcrowded.

The superficial space of six feet by two and a half or three feet appears to us too small even in the loftiest decks, and we think that the height between decks ought to be made an element in the calculation, even when the ventilation is most perfect. We must add, however, that in estimating the number of patients which a vessel can accommodate, mere measurements, whether superficial or cubic, are not the only legitimate elements of computation. The character and gravity of the maladies under which the patients are suffering, or the injuries which they have sustained, the length of time that they are to remain on board, the state of the ventilation, and the season of the year in which the voyage is performed—all these circumstances should be taken into consideration.

The supply of medical attendance on board has not always been sufficient. It is impossible, indeed, to determine exactly, à priori, what number of patients may be properly attended by one surgeon. This number must depend upon the character of the cases to be treated; severe wounds, for instance, obviously exacting more time and care than trifling indispositions. Considering, however, the general nature of the cases, both medical and surgical, that arrived at Scutari during our residence at that place, we think that a surgeon could not give to more than 100 patients daily, even for a short voyage of two or three days, that degree of attendance which a patient should obtain from a medical man. When a larger number was entrusted to his care, we think that the supply of medical attendance was insufficient.

The consequences of this defective supply were, that the medical men were overtaxed, and compelled in some instances to confine their services to the more serious cases on board. Upon this subject we may refer to the evidence of Corporal Buchanan, of the 19th Regiment, who came here on board the "Colombo" in September last. He states that the three surgeons were employed night and day in attending the wounded; and yet that he was obliged to dress his own wound, a slight one in the calf of the leg, from want of medical attendance. We believe that in this, and other vessels which were insufficiently supplied with medical officers, similar cases may have occurred.

Having heard that maggots had been bred, and that this was attributable to the neglect of wounds, we made inquiry upon the subject in various quarters. We questioned an officer whose wound had presented this appearance, and he assured us that he had been properly attended to. Dr. O'Flaherty stated that in three cases he had found maggots in the dressings of wounds which had been dressed within twenty-four hours—two of the cases being officers—and that he had observed the same thing in hospitals at home. Dr. Taylor's evidence is of the same character.

Miss Nightingale informed us that she had found maggots in several cases. In one, an amputation of the thigh, the stump was dressed regularly twice a day. In the other, a compound fracture of both bones of the leg, maggots were found within six hours after a most careful dressing. Without asserting, therefore, that they may not have made their appearance in neglected wounds, we do not regard their presence as an indication that the wounds in which they appeared were neglected; and we did not hear of any case in which their presence was attributed or appeared attributable to neglect. We may add, that the phenomenon is by no means a rare one, but is familiar to surgeons who have served in warm climates.

The number of orderlies sent on board to attend upon the sick and wounded has been almost invariably insufficient. Some vessels, as the "Arthur the Great", the "Orient", the "Caduceus" and the "Sidney", were sent to sea without a single attendant; while on board of others, such as the "Kangaroo", the "Courier", the "Arabia", the "Colombo", the "Edendale" and the "Palmerston", the number sent was merely nominal, and utterly disproportioned to that of the patients. In but few instances has the number allowed by the rules of the service (one in ten) been sent, and in still fewer have all the men employed been fit for duty. Indeed a memorandum issued from head quarters on the 18th October directed that the number to be sent on board transports should be 4 in 100; a number, in our opinion, wholly inadequate for the service on which the men were employed. It would be insufficient if the men had been in strong health, and accustomed to the arduous duties cast upon them; but they have been generally selected from the invalid depôt at

Balaklava; and from bad health, and liability to sea sickness, as well as from want of training, they have not been properly suited for their employment. In numerous instances they fell sick on board, and became, in consequence, an incumbrance instead of an assistance.

Those who were fit for duty were, until December last, under no efficient control. The medical officer had no authority whatever over them, and had no other remedy, in the case of misconduct, than that of reporting them to the military authorities on his arrival at Scutari. A military officer, however, has been sent on board of all vessels which have sailed from Balaklava since the beginning of December. One or more non-commissioned officers have also been sent with the orderlies, and we believe that order has been better maintained by this means. The power of the military officer is very limited, and might be extended with advantage.

With respect to the supply of hospital furniture on board ship, we think that it has not been in general sufficient. A comparison of the number of mattresses and blankets supplied on board each vessel with that of the patients, will not, indeed, give, in our opinion, an exact measure of this deficiency; for we think that in slight cases, whether medical or surgical, the want of a mattress is probably not the legitimate subject of complaint with men accustomed for many months to sleep on the ground and under canvass. In many cases, also, as in violent diarrhœa and dysentery, a mattress becomes unfit for use in the course of a few hours, and might properly be dispensed with. With all due allowance, however, for such cases, we are of opinion, after having inspected several vessels with sick on board, and become acquainted with the general character of the cases which have been brought down from the Crimea, that the supply of mattresses was in general deficient.

The supply of blankets has in general been sufficient; every soldier was provided, with rare exceptions, with his own field blanket, or two blankets.

The supply of hospital utensils and the ordinary appliances for meals appears to have been almost uniformly deficient. Latterly this want has been to some extent remedied; but we think that, with few exceptions, the supply has not been equal to the emergency.

The ventilation of the vessels has been almost uniformly dependent upon scuttles and hatchways. During fine weather these are in general sufficient for the supply of fresh air, but in rough weather the scuttles must necessarily be closed, and then the ventilation of the decks becomes defective.

The means of cooking have in many cases been insufficient. With few exceptions the supply of water has been good.

Except in a few instances, the supply of surgical appliances, medicines, and medical comforts has been represented to us as sufficient, and we have no reason to doubt those representations. The ship's stores have been frequently available for the purposes of the sick and wounded; and although we think it probable that men have occasionally had reason to complain both of the quantity supplied and the manner in which their food was cooked, we are disposed to attribute these faults to the want of order, rather than to the want of a due supply of provisions or medical comforts.

A considerable space of time has on some occasions elapsed between the embarkation of the sick and the commencement of the voyage. Many days elapsed between the first embarkation of sick and wounded on board the "Echunga", the "Tynemouth", the "Shooting Star", the "Arabia", the "Edendale", the "Medway", the "Avon", the "Timandra" and the "Australian", and the sailing of those vessels for their destination. This was owing partly to boisterous weather, but more generally to the fact that the sick were brought down to the harbour in small numbers daily, and the vessels were detained until they had received their complements. The "Australian" appears to have been detained in discharging her cargo, which she was doing while the sick were being sent on board.

The length of time between the first embarkation and the final disembarkation has been in many cases very great. In three instances it exceeded three weeks; in six others it exceeded a fortnight. It has amounted frequently to ten days, and has rarely been less than a week.

The mortality on board has been very high. In the "Caduceus", out of 430 men, 114 died in six days.

This vessel was filled with patients chiefly suffering from Asiatic cholera. In many other instances, however, the mortality, though not so great, has been nevertheless high, and this we believe is in some measure attributable to the length of time during which the men have been kept on board. We regret to add, that the rate of mortality on board continued high down to the end of January, and this we think is partly owing, also, to the more aggravated forms of disease which have appeared among the men, and also to the fact that their constitutions have been impaired by those causes to which Dr. Hall attributes the increase of sickness since last November:—severe duty, exposure, want of vegetable food, want of means of cooking, want of shelter, and, until latterly (Dr. Hall was speaking on the 16th January), want of clothing. We are happy, however, to state that a marked diminution in the mortality is now observable. On board the "Melbourne", which arrived on the 11th of February with 170 sick, two men died, while the "Brandon", which arrived two days later with 118 men, lost only one man.

The equipment of the two vessels first-mentioned, and, we are informed, of two others—the "Australian" and the "Sidney"—as hospital ships, relieves us from the task of offering any suggestions upon this portion of the subject, beyond recommending that both the medical officers and the orderlies should be permanently attached to the vessels, and that the embarkation, voyage, and disembarkation should always be performed with all practicable speed. The "Melbourne" is the only one of these vessels which we have had the opportunity of inspecting. She appears to us to possess all the substantial requisites for the service on which she is engaged. She is fitted up with standing bed places projecting at right angles from the sides of the ship. The bedding consists of thick wadded Turkish coverlets, which answer very well as mattresses, large bolsters, and a proper supply of blankets and rugs. The supply of hospital utensils is sufficient; and besides a large stern cabin used as a surgery, and amply provided with surgical appliances and medicines, the vessel is stored with an abundance of medical comforts.

Within their report to Parliament, the Commissioners included a number of statements by individual soldiers.

ARCHIBOLD MCNICOL, Private 55th Regt.

I volunteered from 92nd to 55th; I was wounded at Alma. I had been about three quarters of an hour engaged. I was struck on the side with a piece of a shell. I crawled to the back of a house which was near, and I lay there for the whole of that day. One hospital was formed at the house next day, and Dr. Cowan, of the 55th, dressed my wound. They got some boiled meat for us, and attended to the worst cases as well as they could. On the forenoon of the 22nd I was carried on a stretcher on board the Arthur the Great (a sailing vessel) by sailors; they carried me very carefully, they did not shake me. I saw many men carried in the country carts driven by the natives: they were not so well off as those who were taken care of by the sailors. They carried me, down into the deck. I got a mattress, and so did all those who went below. I suppose there were 150 below; some also were put into the cabins. Those who were obliged to remain on deck had no mattresses. I was on the deck several times during the passage, and could see whether they had mattresses or not. They were served out with extra blankets. I had only my own blanket, and that was taken from me to roll up a man who had died next me, and then I got another blanket, a new one. My blanket was on the deck, and touched on each side that of my neighbour. It was very close—bad smell, very—the smell of wounds and filth. The ship was well enough ventilated, but there was no one to clean up the place, and that was the chief occasion of the smell. The doctor saw me the evening I went on board. There were a few sick, but we were chiefly wounded. There were a good many operations on board. They used chloroform in some cases. The doctor came round once a day. I heard many of the men complain that they were not attended to. There were no orderlies except a few who were slightly wounded, and who assisted their comrades. The only conveniences were ship's buckets large and small, and the sailors came down occasionally and assisted in carrying away and emptying them.

There were about twenty soldiers' wives; they were very active in assisting, and dressing the men's wounds, until some got sick.

The cholera broke out after we had been three or four days on board, and a great many men died, some from that, and some from wounds.

There was plenty of meat given out if we had only had the means of having it distributed. There was one sergeant of the 1st Royals who was on board in charge of the knapsacks of his regiment; he, and some slightly wounded distributed the food. It was pretty well cooked. There was both salt and fresh—that is, preserved meat. There was also sago. No porter or wine. Those who acted as orderlies got grog, nobody else. The meals were very irregular. We sometimes got tea at 11 p.m. We arrived on the 26th.

When I got ashore, I was assisted up to the hospital by two men; that was in the forenoon. I got no bed that day. I slept with my great coat and blanket in the corridor. It was fine weather and I felt no cold. My wound was not attended to that day. I never asked, because my wound was a slight one, and I knew there were many severe cases. Next day I got a mattress and pillow, blanket, and rug. My wound was properly dressed; it was dressed with a piece of lint. I was only six days in hospital. I then became an orderly, caught the fever, and went into hospital. This time I got a bedstead, boards and trestles. It was the 9th of the month. I got every thing comfortable. Diet is good, and I get all I require. I have never given my shirts to be washed by the hospital; a soldier's wife washes my things for me. I bought shirts myself after I got pay. I lost all my things here. They came on board the ship. I do not know whether they left the ship, but I have never seen them since.

There was no regular pack-store at the time; the packs were put into a ward near the place where Miss Nightingale now lives, and anybody who liked might go in, that is, any soldier who was passed in by a corporal. Everything was knocked about and in a state of confusion.

SAMUEL WELLS, Coldstream Guards.

I lost my arm on the 24th November [1854]. It was shattered to pieces by the fall of some ten tons of small-arm ammunition, that I and a fatigue party were putting up in a chamber in a windmill near the first division. The French encampment was within 100 yards, and the French ran up and helped us out. About twenty were in the mill. They carried me to the general hospital of the first division. The general doctor and another looked at me there, and as they said the arm must come off, the French carried me off to our own hospital tents. They carried me in one of the English ambulances. I got there about 11.30 a.m. I had got very faint and low. They amputated my arm about 5 p.m. There was no table; I sat on a medicine chest. They did not give me chloroform. After the amputation, they put me on a trestle bedstead, with five blankets, two underneath and three on top. I was there 13 days; I came away on the thirteenth morning. I was carried on a commissariat cart; we call them Malta cars. It shook me very bad. There were one man both sick and wounded, and one wounded, besides, in the car. We went on board at once; that was on the 7th December. The vessel was in the harbour. We were four or five days before sailing. The men on board were chiefly sick. I think some men were on board the day before I went on board. During the four or five days we were in harbour fresh sick men came in daily. We were fourteen days between going on board and landing. We lay for four days within a mile of the mouth of the Bosphorous, until they sent a steamer for us. I landed among the first on the following day.

I saw no mattresses on board at all; I did not get one. I went throughout the vessel. Every man had an extra blanket besides his own. Some very bad cases, chiefly sick, about twelve in number, got two extra blankets. We all lay on the deck, with our heads to the sides of the vessel. We lay very close to each other— just room to turn, nothing more. The air was very foul in the night; it was not quite so bad in the day, as many could get on deck. The foul smell was owing to so many men having diarrhœa and lying so close. There were enough utensils to enable the orderlies to relieve the men, and they generally managed to relieve them pretty well. But they sometimes got lazy—I mean the orderlies—and lay still when men called. We had two for every mess of 19.

Convalescents, also, assisted. The doctors attended very well, twice a day, and came also at any call when an orderly went to call them. We lost 23 coming down, only one of them wounded. We had 227 at starting.

We had enough to eat. The men on full diet got ship's rations; the bad cases got sago and seaman's dough, port wine. All got either port wine or grog; in bad cases, men got two gills of wine. I heard of no want of medicines. My arm was dressed every other day. The doctor came to me every day. My arm was going on very well, and did not require dressing oftener. It is dressed here every other day. The meals were well managed, but rather late.

We had a military officer on board in charge, Captain Maxwell, 88th. He came down and looked once or twice a day, to see if the place was kept clean, whether there were any complaints, and whether the orderlies did their duty. I think that kept them to their duty. I heard the men in some messes say that if the orderlies had not been looked after, they would have been very bad indeed.

When I landed I was taken straight away to a ward in the Barrack hospital. That might have been about 3 p.m. The doctor saw me at about 6 p.m., at his evening visit. He asked me about my health, and where my arm had been dressed. He did not look at it. He dressed it on the second morning. I had not a bedstead, but a mattress on the Turkish divan that goes round the ward. I got blankets, rug, sheets, and a pillow. I feel comfortable in every respect. I get my victuals warm and comfortable—no reason whatever to complain. Almost every man is served out with some wine every day. There are six or seven wounded; the rest are diarrhœa and dysentery. I had a flannel shirt given to me, and this morning the doctor took down my name for flannel drawers and socks, and another shirt.

PART 3

∞⚬⚬∞

*From the Parliamentary Commissioners' report into the
condition of the hospitals at Scutari.*

∘⊶❦⊷∘

Description of hospital accommodation.

When the transport arrives off Scutari, the sick and wounded are landed. Much delay, however, has frequently occurred in completing the disembarkation. This was at first mainly attributable to the difficulty, to which we shall have occasion presently to advert, in landing at the hospital wharf except in calm weather, and in some instances also to the want of the requisite supply of boats. Since the middle of December last, it has been caused principally by the crowded state of the hospitals, which were not always prepared to afford immediate accommodation to the patients on board.

Upon landing, those who are unable to walk are carried on stretchers, by fatigue parties, either of our own men or of Turks. We have observed more confusion than is desirable in effecting this landing, and we think that the patients might be distributed in the wards with less delay than frequently occurs. On their arrival at the hospital to which they are allotted, the clothes, packs, and arms of the patients are carried to the pack store.

The situation of the hospitals at Scutari is healthy, but in other respects it is open to objection. The shore of the sea of Marmora, near which the buildings stand, is comparatively shallow. Two small piers, one near the barrack, the other near the General Hospital, offer facilities for disembarkation from open boats and even from small steamers in calm weather; but during the prevalence of S. and S. W. winds, the sea on the shore renders this accommodation wholly unavailable. The late Mr. Ward, the purveyor, and Mr. Potgieter, the Deputy Assistant Commissary General at Scutari, informed us that in some instances boats loaded with clothing and baggage had been swamped in attempting to land at the hospital wharfs, which indeed are very insufficient. The nearest landing places, when these are inaccessible, are the wharfs of Scutari and Kadikoi, which are each about a mile and a half distant from the Barrack Hospital, and difficult to reach from that building, owing to the want of good roads. Under these circumstances, the hospitals at Scutari are frequently cut off from the market from which they derive their principal supplies— Constantinople. Great delay, also, arises from the same cause in getting on shore the stores which are brought out from England, and similar delay as frequently occurs both in landing the sick and wounded men who are sent down from the Crimea, and in embarking drafts destined for home or for the seat of war. It has been suggested to us, that these disadvantages are in some measure counterbalanced by the removal of our soldiers from the contaminating influences of a large town population such as exists in Constantinople; but it seems to us probable that those influences are quite as active in the large town or suburb of Scutari as they would be found in the capital itself.

To the disadvantages of situation which we have above indicated, the magnitude and conveniences of the principal buildings which have been appropriated as hospitals for the use of our army may perhaps be regarded as a sufficient set-off. The edifices near Scutari at present occupied in this capacity by the sick and wounded of our army are four in number. First, a barrack erected by the Sultan Selim for Turkish troops; 2nd, the hospital; 3rd, the stables attached to the barrack; and, 4th, a palace called Haidar Pasha.

The barrack is a quadrilateral building, with turrets at the external angles. It is of great size; its two longest sides being 220 yards long, and its shorter, 194 yards. It is situated on a ridge, which inclines downwards towards the S., E., and W., and the erection has been so adapted to the shape of the ground that the storey which, at the main entrance on the north or upper side, is the ground floor, becomes, as it extends to the right and left and to the other sides of the building, the first, and a little further on, the second floor. Above this ground floor is another which extends along a portion of it only. Below the storey which we have called the ground floor lie two others, commencing at a little distance on each side of the main entrance. One half only, however, of the upper of these two floors is at present occupied by sick and wounded. The other half, and the whole of the lowest storey, are occupied by the depot, or given up to the Ordnance, Commissariat, and Purveyor's departments, for stores. The several floors are connected by large stone staircases, which have very spacious landing places. There are two of these staircases on each of three sides, and one on the fourth or east side.

With the exception of the eastern and one half of the southern sides, the building was in good repair when we first inspected it in November last. The portions above mentioned were then in a state of dilapidation, and were not put into tenantable repair until from the middle of December to the middle of January last. This was done by the engineers' department, by the direction of the British Ambassador, who furnished the requisite funds for the purpose.

The general arrangement of the apartments is well adapted for hospital purposes. It consists of a series of rooms occupying about two thirds of the entire depth of the building, and placed on its external side. They open upon a corridor which runs round the inner portion of it. The rooms vary in size; but they are, in general, large and lofty. The smaller ones, which were constructed for officers' quarters, have a servants' room, pantry, and privy generally attached to them. The large rooms, intended for soldiers' barrack rooms, are skirted by a low wooden sleeping bench, differing from that of our own guard rooms only in its being horizontal. Both the rooms and the corridors are amply lighted and ventilated by numerous windows, and are heated by stoves, which were placed in them during the months of November and December last by the engineers' department. At the four inner angles of the building are extensive privies of the ordinary Turkish construction. Each corridor has access to them at its two extremities. They are sufficient in number, but are not adapted to the habits of Europeans, and are in consequence often in a most offensive state. A fatigue party of Turks and Armenians is employed daily in cleansing them; but this duty has been in general very imperfectly performed. The upper storey of the north side of the quadrangle, which we have described as not extending over the entire length of that side of the building, is wholly destitute of this kind of accommodation. The means of ablution are situated in anterooms to these places.

In the lowest floor there is a kitchen, used only by the depôt. Within the quadrangle several wooden huts have been recently erected. We think that the site was injudiciously selected, for the structures impede the circulation of air through the barracks, and their occupants will receive but a vitiated atmosphere, which they will corrupt still further, to the injury of the inmates of the main building. In the same quadrangle are two kitchens of considerable dimensions, one of which, however, has not yet been made available, owing to some difficulty in procuring the requisite coppers for fitting it up. The other is supplied with thirteen copper boilers, containing about fifty-six gallons. The boilers are heated by a corresponding number of fire-places, fed at the exterior of the building. As the chimney does not communicate with the apartment, the latter is kept constantly damp by the steam which escapes from the boilers. No means exist in this kitchen of cooking in any other way than boiling.

Besides those which were in existence while the barrack was still in the occupation of the Turks, four supplementary kitchens have been recently constructed—one in the basement, for the exclusive use of sick and wounded officers, and three others for cooking the extra diets of the patients. One of these was constructed in the middle of November, for the use of Miss Nightingale; another, on a landing place, in December; and the last, in the present month.

In other landings surgeries and offices have been established.

The supply of water is good and abundant, but is not as conveniently distributed as would be desirable, there being but two or three places, besides the depôt kitchen, in the entire building, at which it can be drawn.

At a short distance from the building is a wash-house, containing 62 wooden troughs. It was, until the beginning of this month, used as a store by the commissariat, but it is now undergoing repairs, to adapt it to the purpose for which it was erected.

The General Hospital is a quadrilateral building, resembling the Barrack in the general arrangement of its wards and corridors. It is spacious, well lighted, and in tolerable repair. The wards and corridors are heated by stoves, most of which were in the building while it was occupied by the Turks. The ventilation and lighting arrangements are similar to those in the Barrack. The privies, which are situated at the four outer angles of the building, are open to the same remarks as those in the Barrack. The wash-house is furnished with a large fire-place, and with wooden troughs along the two adjoining sides. The stone flooring is broken, and in need of repair. A supply of cold water is laid on close to the fire; but no supply of either cold or hot water is carried to the troughs.

The kitchen was, until lately, very defective, but is now undergoing improvement. It is still but imperfectly lighted by a dome studded with small round panes of glass; and the floor, which is of stone, is uneven, broken, inclining towards the fire-place, and affording lodgment for dirt and wet. The fire-places are fed in the same manner as those of the kitchen in the Barrack Hospital, and are supplied with 11 coppers, 9 of which contain 24 gallons, and the others about 40.

The quadrangle is laid out as a garden, and partially cultivated for the supply of vegetables. In its centre is a large fountain, which affords the means of supplying abundance of water throughout the establishment, but at present the pipes are out of repair. The hospital possesses an excellent Turkish bath house.

The principal stores of the purveyor and apothecary are in this building.

The palace of Haidar Pasha is situated on a lower level than either of the preceding buildings. It lies at the bottom of a valley formed by the ridge on which the General Hospital stands and that on which the town of Kadikoi is built. It is about a mile from the sea of Marmora. It is approached from Scutari and Kadikoi by a roughly-paved road or causeway. It consists of a series of irregular buildings, consisting of a ball-room or theatre, hareem and pavilion. The last-mentioned portion has been occupied but within the last few days. The building is of wood. The rooms are well lighted. They are ventilated by doors and loosely fitting windows, and warmed by stoves. The drainage is defective. Surface water lodges in considerable quantity in the adjoining meadow and road. This, however, may, we believe, be rectified by properly scouring or reconstructing a drain.

The hareem is a building of two storeys; the rooms open from very large landings, on each of which there is a stove.

Near the barrack hospital is a large stable, over part of which there are several rooms, opening on a corridor. These have been used as wards since the 8th of January. The wards are three in number. There are small privies at each end of the corridor, and at each end also are the quarters of the medical officers and the surgery. In the court-yard below is an abundant supply of water, and a kitchen with three coppers, amply sufficient for cooking for the patients in the building. There is no supply of water in the wards.

Besides the several buildings above mentioned, a cavalry barrack, with its hospital, at Kuleli, a town several miles up the Bosphorous, has been recently occupied by the sick and wounded of the army. The barrack is built close to the water's edge, under a precipitous cliff.

It consists of six lofty wards, with galleries nine feet wide. These apartments are well suited for hospital purposes, with the exception of the galleries, which, although well ventilated with windows, should, we think, be very sparingly used as dormitories, as they necessarily receive the heated and vitiated air from below.

The barrack has a good kitchen, supplied with seven large boilers, heated in the same manner as those of the hospitals at Scutari. It possesses also a wash-house, containing twelve marble troughs, each of which is supplied with cold water. There is also a fountain at one end of the apartment. Adjoining it is a Turkish bath-house.

The privies are of the usual Turkish construction,

and are open to the observations which we have already made respecting those in the hospitals at Scutari.

Under one of the first-mentioned wards is a stable, the effluvium from which must necessarily be injurious to the patients.

The building which was appropriated as a hospital for the troops quartered in this barrack has also been occupied by us. It is a large square building, containing on the upper storey seven wards, opening on corridors. Below this storey is another, consisting of three wards, and of a corridor which is not occupied; and there is another in a still lower floor. The lower storey is wholly unsuited for the accommodation of patients.

This hospital is provided with a kitchen, containing six large boilers, and with an excellent wash-house, supplied with seven troughs. Adjoining to the latter are a drying room, a small apartment in which water is laid on for a boiler, and a small Turkish bath-house.

We have to notice a striking want in every one of the hospital establishments here, which has been much felt by the medical officers, and which admits of easy remedy. No room has been set apart in any of the hospitals, except the General Hospital, for operations. These are necessarily performed in the wards, and in the presence of other patients. Another want felt by the profession is the utter absence of sufficient accommodation for post mortem examinations.

oocoℰ◆☉oo

The hospital attendants (including Florence Nightingale and her staff).

The orderlies have in point of numbers been always amply sufficient. In every other respect, however, except that of mere numbers, we regard this branch of the hospital service as most unsatisfactory. The orderlies are drawn from the ranks, without any regard to their aptitude or their inclination for the employment, and are mostly men whose weak constitution unfits them for the hardships of a campaign, or convalescents who have not sufficiently recovered their health to return to active service. The duties of a hospital orderly are frequently distasteful to them; and the low rate of pay, 4d. a day, is not a sufficient inducement to them to overcome their repugnance. They are also liable to be sent back to their regiments; and their places are then filled by men of the same character, without the advantage of the experience which their predecessors acquired. We must add that the general habits of our soldiers do not peculiarly qualify them for a situation requiring great steadiness of conduct; and from the rank of life to which they belong, and the terms of intimacy which naturally subsist between themselves and their patients, they have never the authority to prevent, and seldom the inclination to report, any irregularities which may come under their notice.

The ward-masters and assistant ward-masters are generally intelligent and respectable non-commissioned officers; but they do not possess that degree of experience in the duties of their office which ought, in our opinion, to be an indispensable condition to their employment in such a capacity in our military hospitals. The cooks, also, are soldiers; and although they may be useful as assistants, we think that they are but indifferently acquainted with the peculiar style of cooking required in hospitals.

The pack-storekeepers are non-commissioned officers, but, like all other soldiers, are liable to be ordered off to their regiments.

Besides the above hospital attendants, we have to notice the staff of female nurses under the superin-

tendence of Miss Nightingale. That lady arrived at
Scutari on the 4th November, accompanied by
thirty-eight nurses. These are employed to attend to
such cases as the medical officers in charge, and the
staff surgeons of their divisions, concur in considering
cases requiring such attendance. They are employed
chiefly, according to Miss Nightingale's evidence,
among the wounded, the operation cases, and the
severe medical cases. Their duties consist, in surgical
cases, in washing, and preparing for the morning visits of the medical officer, such wounds as they are
directed by that officer to treat in this way; to attend
upon him in dressing the wounds; and to receive, and
take to Miss Nightingale, his directions as to diet,
drink, and medical comforts. In surgical cases, a corridor and two wards are generally assigned to four
nurses. In medical cases, their duties consist in dressing bed-sores, seeing that the food of the patients is
properly cooked and properly administered, and that
cleanliness, both of the wards and of the person, is
attended to. We have reason to believe that the services of these hospital attendants have been extremely
valuable.

Concerning the supplies of medicines and medical equipment in the hospitals.

With respect to the supply of medicines, hospital furniture, medical comforts, and provisions in these hospitals, we regret to state that the information which we have been able to collect is most unsatisfactory.

The first step which we took on entering upon the inquiry directed by our Commission was to write to the apothecary and the chief purveyor at Scutari for a return of the several articles which were in their stores on the 1st of September last, of the articles received by them subsequently to that date, distinguishing from what quarters these had been obtained, and of the daily issues from their stores down to the day of the date of our letters, the 28th November.

We regret to state that we failed to procure the particulars thus applied for. The apothecary was suddenly seized with illness about the date of our letter, and died within a day or two after. As his successor did not furnish us with the returns in question within a reasonable time, we made a personal inspection of the stores and books; and having come to the conclusion, from the state of both, that the information, if attainable at all, would not be attained without much delay, we were compelled to resort to another and much less satisfactory mode of ascertaining whether the supply of medicines and surgical appliances had been sufficient or not.

We proceeded, accordingly, to examine in the middle of December, every surgeon who was still doing duty, and who was in the hospital about the time when the wounded from the battle of the Alma arrived. Those gentlemen were fourteen in number; viz., Doctors Menzies, M'Grigor, Ancell, Sunter, Wishart, Hungerford, Reid, Tydd, Evans, M'Munn, Wood, Hamilton, Johnson, and Calder. We also examined Mr. Darrac and Mr. Andrews, the dispensers at the General and Barrack hospitals during the same period. The conclusion to which all this evidence would, *per se*, lead is, that from the time of the arrival of the wounded in September, until the date of their

examination, there was no want of surgical appliances, with the exception of the double incline plane,
or M'Intyre's splints, used occasionally for compound
fractures of the leg, of which there was not a sufficient
supply; of oil silk for about two days in the middle of
November last; and of tow on one occasion, when the
more expensive material, charpie, was used in its
place. As it had been generally rumoured that lint and
old linen, and other such appliances, had been wanting for dressing the wounds of the men who had
been brought to the hospital after the engagement of
the 20th September we directed the attention of our
witnesses more specially to those articles, but we did
not elicit that any such want had been experienced.

The evidence of the same gentlemen also would
tend to show that the supply of medicines was always
sufficient during the same period, with the exception
of nitric acid, which was wanting for about forty-
eight hours in the beginning of December, and for
which chloride of antimony was used; of bicarbonate
of soda, which was wanting for about the same length
of time, towards the middle of November; and of
powdered opium, for about the same space of time,
on one or two occasions, for which the various other
preparations of that drug were substituted.

We subsequently obtained from Miss Nightingale
a list of apothecaries' stores supplied by her since her
arrival at Scutari [not supplied here]. This table—
coupled with Miss Nightingale's statement, that she
did not issue any of the articles which it contained
without having first been assured by the apothecary

that they were not in store, and were not expected—as well as the evidence of the medical officers to which we have above referred, would, under ordinary circumstances, afford strong evidence that the stores which failed to supply the articles in question were destitute of them. We hesitated, however, from the knowledge we had acquired by personal inspection of these stores, to adopt this inference, and subsequent inquiry satisfied us that any such inference would be unsafe.

With the view of testing the reasonableness of our doubts, we procured from the office of the Principal Medical Officer the return of the stock taken by a Board which was lately appointed to take stock of the apothecary's stores.

This return is dated the 5th February. Upon examining the file of requisitions on those stores between the 1st and 10th of February, we find that several medicines were refused, although they were, according to the return of the Board, in the stores on the 5th of the same month.

These few instances will suffice to show the fallacy of inferring from the refusal of articles required that they were not in store. Our observations, however, should not be understood as casting blame on any individuals, for such is neither their aim nor their necessary effect. The want of storage-room, both in the General and the Barrack hospitals, may perhaps account in some measure for the confusion which we have noticed. Upon the whole, we come to the conclusion that although it is not impossible that some of the surgical appliances and medicines mentioned by the medical officers whom we have above named, and by Miss Nightingale, may have been wanting on two or three occasions during the last five months, yet in the absence of positive and precise evidence on the subject we are unable to specify either their precise nature or extent. We think it right, however, to add that the Barrack hospital has, to our own immediate knowledge, been left unsupplied on more than one occasion with articles in store, owing to the neglect to keep the surgeries properly furnished.

With respect to the adequacy of the supply of hospital furniture, clothing, and medical comforts, we have been equally unsuccessful in obtaining the information which we demanded, or any other evidence of a sufficiently precise character to enable us to arrive at an exact conclusion upon the subject. From the evidence of Mr. Sabin and others, there appears to have been a great want of bedsteads, mattresses, bedding, and hospital utensils, when the wounded arrived in September, and the want of bedsteads has continued to be felt to the present time. At present the furniture of the hospital appears tolerably complete. With the exception of some bedsteads still wanting at Haidar Pasha, we do not notice any want of hospital furniture. At Kuleli the bedsteads are provided with shelves at the head, in imitation of the French hospital bedstead, and this arrangement contributes much to order in the wards.

For the purpose of obtaining a more exact view of the deficiencies of this department of the hospital establishment than is afforded by evidence of this general character, we applied to Miss Nightingale for some returns, which she was good enough to furnish to us. It is only necessary to premise, that that lady, shortly after her arrival at Scutari, commenced to supply the hospital with articles of furniture, clothing, and medical comforts.

Her store, it will be seen, was supplied partly from the public, but chiefly from her own private resources, and the issues were made solely on the requisitions of medical officers in charge of wards, countersigned by the staff surgeon of the division. The issues of clothing and furniture were made, also, only after Miss Nightingale had ascertained from the purveyor that the articles demanded were not in store, and that he did not expect them from England or Constantinople.

We also made a similar application to Mr. Macdonald, a gentleman who has been engaged, both here and in the Crimea, for the last three months, in expending a large charitable fund, placed at the disposal of the proprietors of "The Times" newspaper, for the benefit of the sick and wounded soldiers of the British Army in the East; and that gentleman readily consented to furnish us with a list of the articles which he had supplied, as well to the hospitals of Scutari as to those of Balaklava and the field, and to the transport ships; but, having learned from him that he had not, like Miss Nightingale, inquired of the purveyors, before sending his donations to their destination, whether the goods were in store or expected, we found that the information which we

List of the principal Articles of HOSPITAL FURNITURE, &c. supplied by F. NIGHTINGALE, on the Requisitions of the Medical Officers, to the Hospitals of SCUTARI, from 10th November 1854 to 15th February 1855.

No. supplied.		Obtained from Public Stores	Obtained from Public Sources
*10,537	Cotton shirts	400	10,137
*6,823	Flannel shirts	400	6,423
*4,607	Drawers	—	4,607
6,173	Prs. socks and stockings	50	6,123
1,508	Nightcaps	270	1,238
1,350	Prs. slippers	300	1,050
*2,674	Comforters	—	2,674
*427	Prs. mits	—	427
443	Hospital suits of clothing	150	293
*615	Handkerchiefs	—	615
*301	Flannel belts	—	301
379	Sheets	379	—
Ad libitum	Old linen sheets	—	2,000
*789	Towels	150	639
*20	Hair mattresses	20	—
*247	Hair pillows	—	247
150	Straw pillows	150	—
715	Knives and forks	70	645
1,117	Spoons	100	1,017
4,326	Drinking-cups (tin)	300	4,026
557	Drinking-cups (earthenware)	57	500
1,786	Plates (tin)	300	1,486
75	Meat dishes	—	75
*155	Basins (zinc)	—	155
*280	Basins (earthenware)	80	200

No. supplied.		Obtained from Public Stores	Obtained from Public Sources
★100	Basins (wooden)	—	100
319	Bedpans	—	319
270	Urinals	—	270
24	Close-stools and pans	—	24
★28	Buckets	—	28
★192	Tin pails for soup	—	192
★86	Wooden trays	—	86
75	Hair brooms	30	45
136	Hand scrubbers	—	136
78	Long scrubbers	—	78
48	Mops	48	—
★93 sets	Shoe brushes	—	93 sets.
★22½ dozen	Blacking	—	22½ dozen.
★528	Combs	444	84
★106	Lamps and lanterns	—	106
★51	Prs. scissors	—	51
★39	Mats (cocoa nut)	—	39
27	Saucepans	10	17
1	Boiler	1	—
36	Candlesticks	—	36
★24	Sick-feeders	—	24
20	Expectorating cups	—	20
138	Gallipots	138	—
84	Tables	—	84
144	Forms	—	144
★19	Clocks	—	19
16	Baths	—	16
★2	Operating tables	—	2

★ The articles marked with an asterisk form no part of the hospital furniture and clothing, according to the regulations of the service.

demanded was unavailable for the purpose for which we desired it, viz., as a test of the deficiency of the purveyors' stores.

Having regard to the inquiry made of the purveyors before the issue of the articles here set forth, and having no reason for believing that any disorder prevailed in their offices, the above list would, *prima facie*, tend strongly to prove that the public stores were not always kept duly supplied since November last with the articles described as being derived from private sources.

It fails, however, to prove the whole extent of the deficiency, for Miss Nightingale's supplies were not always equal to the demands upon them; nor does it afford any indication of the deficiency of any other articles which Miss Nightingale did not furnish.

On the other hand, it must be observed that a considerable number of the articles furnished by Miss Nightingale form no part of the ordinary hospital furniture. But further, confining ourselves to such goods as do, according to the hospital regulations, form a part of such furniture, the list must not be regarded as conclusive proof that the articles mentioned in it were invariably wanting in the stores, for goods have been refused, although they were, to our personal knowledge, lying in abundance in the store of the purveyor. This was done because they had not been examined by a Board of Survey. On one occasion in December we found that this was the case with hospital rugs, and it is probable that this has not been the only instance of such an occurrence.

As a further means of ascertaining, if not the extent of the deficiencies in the purveyors' furniture and clothing stores, at least the nature of the articles which have been from time to time wanting, we requested to see the file of requisitions kept in the purveyors' offices in the Barrack and General hospitals since October last. To explain the bearing of these documents upon the question, it is necessary to state that articles of hospital furniture and clothing are issued by the purveyor only upon written demands. If he is wholly unable to comply with a requisition when it is presented, he returns the document to the bearer; but if he can supply some of the articles demanded, he retains and files it, striking out, often in pencil merely, those articles which he is unable to furnish. The file of requisitions, therefore, does not faithfully represent the whole of the wants of the hospital. It does not show the whole quantity of articles refused, nor perhaps even all the various kinds of such articles, but indicates merely that some articles which were demanded at the same time as others could not be supplied.

An examination of the lists of articles which we found struck out in the requisitions between October and January, both inclusive, will show some of the wants which were not supplied when required; but, for the reason which we have stated, we attach little value to the trifling evidence which it affords.

Before leaving this subject, we have to express our opinion that the practice of issuing articles on requisition is very objectionable, and should be limited as far as practicable to the supply of casual and unforeseen wants. According to the "Instructions of the Purveying Department of the Army of the East," of 14th November last, bedding, dresses, and utensils are to be issued to the steward on demands duly approved by the senior medical officer; but the time of the steward is so wholly engaged, as we shall presently show, in dealing out provisions, that he is unable to attend to any other branch of his duties. The task of making these demands, and consequently of inquiring into the state of the supply of such articles in the wards, is in practice thrown, in these establishments, on the medical officers in charge of wards, whose requisitions, as we have already noticed, need the countersignature of the staff surgeon of the division. We think that this duty should not be cast upon the medical officers. It is, in our opinion, an evil that the wards of a hospital are not furnished with their periodical supply of sheets, shirts, and even of fuel or candles, or obtain their full complements of bedsteads, bedding, and other articles of furniture, without a formality which encroaches upon the time and interferes with the legitimate duties of medical men. We think that all such wants ought to be inquired into, or rather periodically anticipated, by the officer whose duty it is to supply them.

From the neglect to file those requisitions which are altogether rejected, coupled with the practice of never issuing articles except upon written demands, it sometimes happens, that while wards are in want of articles, a quantity of these is lying in store, and might be had upon application. We found this to be the case on more than one occasion in the course of our inquiry. The following instance may be mentioned. It may be seen, upon reference to the list of furniture in the purveyor's store on 31st January, that there were on that day a number of boards and trestles in store, and yet, upon inquiring, a few days later, we ascertained that there were still wanting in the Barrack hospital alone 289 bedsteads, viz., 142 in the first division, 87 in the second, and 60 in the third, to complete its furniture; while in Haidar Pasha a considerable number of patients was still unsupplied.

It is not to be inferred that the surgeons neglect to make the wants of their wards known. This state of things is the result of the omission to make a note or memorandum, when a requisition is not answered, of the article demanded, and of the person demanding it—an omission which leaves the purveyor without the means of furnishing the goods when his store is replenished, but compels him to wait for a fresh requisition. We have been assured that steps are taken to give due notice of the arrival of goods which have been in demand; but we believe that those steps have been very ineffectual. We have found that surgeons whose requisitions were not complied with when they were made, have remained long in ignorance that their demands might be supplied if repeated. On the other hand, the refusal which they have met becomes generally known, and requisitions for the article in question cease to be made. We believe that many deficiencies which have been at different times observed in the furniture of the wards is to be attributed to the practice of issuing only upon requisition, and to the neglect to supply at a subsequent time those requisitions which were not immediately answered.

In support of the practice of issuing upon requisition, it is said that those documents are necessary, or at least convenient, as vouchers to prove that the articles mentioned in them have been supplied; but we think that in this respect their value is worthless, because it must constantly be optional with the purveyor or clerk receiving the requisition whether he shall or not draw his pen or pencil through those articles which he is unable to supply. In this respect a receipt by the recipient after the article has been furnished is of far superior value and effect. We think it right, after making this observation, to add, that we have not the slightest ground for suspecting that any such fraud as we have alluded to as of possible occurrence, has even been attempted; but, in pointing out the evils of the system, we do not think it right to omit all notice of such a defect. For the above reasons, we think that the practice of issuing on requisition is vicious, and should be limited as much as possible.

A return [not given here], which we obtained a few days ago, shows the quantity of hospital furniture in the purveyor's store at Scutari on the 31st January. This was before the arrival of the "Eagle", freighted with a large cargo of articles for the use of the hospitals, including, among other things, 27,000 cotton shirts.

In order to form an opinion of the adequacy of these supplies to meet future demands, it is necessary to bear in mind that the stores at Scutari are intended to meet all the wants, not only of the Barrack and the General hospitals, the Stables, Haidar Pasha, the Hulk, the "Bombay", and the establishments at Kuleli, Abydos, Smyrna, and Gallipoli, but also to some extent those at Balaklava and the hospitals in the field. On the other hand, it may be important to observe, that a vast quantity of hospital furniture is at present in use, and that that quantity may suffice for future demands, if the number of patients should decrease. In judging, however, of the probable wants of our military hospitals, we possess no sufficient grounds for calculating upon any diminution in the numbers under medical treatment. We therefore think it probable that the supply of hospital furniture and clothing, with the exception of blankets, sheets, and perhaps of two or three other articles, will not be found sufficient for the wants of the sick and wounded.

Immediately connected with the subject of hospital furniture and clothing is the provision which has been made for the washing, both of bedding and personal clothing. This, we are of opinion, has not been satisfactory. At the General Hospital, indeed, eight or ten Armenians are employed for this purpose, and we have heard no complaints from the men there, except that they frequently get the shirt of another instead of their own from the wash; and this we may observe involves a greater evil than the mere loss of property.

The washing is effected without boiling, and without this process it is impossible to get rid of animal matter. Under such circumstances the exchange complained of is peculiarly objectionable. The washing of the bed linen is very badly done there, the sheets which return from the wash being frequently found in a more filthy condition than those which they are intended to replace.

From the information which has been furnished to us by the purveyor, it will be seen that 7,824 shirts were washed at that hospital during the month of January, which gives to every man about two shirts per week. The number washed at the Barrack hospital during the same period was only 3,837; and as the average number of patients in that building exceeded in January 2,200, all the men did not even get one shirt in a fortnight from the public washing establishment.

The washing at the Barrack is done by contract, and not only is the quantity washed in general insufficient, but the washing is very inadequately performed; Miss Nightingale states, in her evidence in February, that she had seen "blankets come back from the wash torn and covered with stains." She added, that she had herself "sorted these blankets when taking in sick, and been compelled to throw away the so-called clean blankets till they could be carried away and destroyed."

Mr. Stuart gave us a similar description of the washing at an earlier period. We must add, that we heard of some shirts having been brought into the wards, on one occasion, as clean which were found on examination with lice upon them; and Dr. Calder states in his evidence the same thing with respect to blankets.

With the view of meeting to some extent the want of proper washing, Miss Nightingale established a wash-house on the 30th November, which was provided with boilers, partly from the engineers' office, partly from her own resources. The average number of articles washed weekly at that establishment during the month of January was 500 shirts and 150 other articles; but these figures, like the other returns which we obtained from the same quarter, do not indicate the whole extent of the evil sought to be remedied. We are glad to state, however, that washing, wringing, and drying machines have arrived from England, for the purpose of doing all the washing of these establishments.

From Miss Nightingale's evidence, it appears that some of the articles [of food and drink] which she supplied from private sources were so supplied, not because the purveyor was unable to furnish the goods in question, but because the quality of those which he procured was not good. This was the case with respect to the chickens, arrow root, milk, port wine, and brandy. The other articles in the list, which were supplied from private sources, were refused to Miss Nightingale on requisition.

With exception of such articles, the observations which we have already made upon the bearing of Miss Nightingale's supplementary assistance to the purveying departments apply.

We think it right to observe, with respect to one important article in the catalogue of medical comforts, viz., port wine, that the quantity which has been used, as we are informed, in these hospitals, has been in our opinion greatly excessive, and wholly disproportioned to the real wants of the sick.

PART 4

∞⊗∞

Statements made by individuals to the Parliamentary Commissioners concerning hospital conditions at Scutari.

∘∘⋘✕⋙∘∘

*From evidence given by the purveyors and military commis-
sariat at Scutari.*

Mr. SELKIRK STUART, Purveyor of Barrack
Hospital.
December 16th

The contractor of the Commissariat supplies meat,
bread, milk, fowls, eggs. The contractor has purchased
wine for us when we have been short. The contractor
is Mr. Parry. Mr. Wreford has also purchased port. We
once got eight cases of port from the contractor. On

another occasion we opened by mistake some cases of Mr. Parry's, which had just been put, for the night, into the purveyor's store. Candles, lamp-oil, rice, sugar, barley, wood, charcoal, and porter we draw from the Commissariat direct on my requisition. The meat comes at about 3 or 4 o'clock on the previous day; the fowls for the day come in the morning, sometimes before 12. There has been a great consumption of fowls; three days ago there were 220 issued. That day order was given for 300. Next morning only 120 could be procured. I inspect the things daily. I have had sometimes to condemn the meat, but not the fowls. They are sometimes small, but we cannot help that. There are never old hens among them.

The diet rolls have been supplied to the steward only between 7 and 8 a.m. of the day that they are to be issued. I think it would be advisable that the purveyor should have an abstract of the diets and extras at three o'clock the previous day. The diet rolls are brought in the morning when the orderlies get their bread: the steward then marks down in his books the total of the diets and bread with the orderly's name. After breakfast the orderlies return for bread and meat for dinner. This issue is interrupted by serving out the supplies for sick officers, and on some occasions the issue has not been completed before a quarter to two o'clock, but I have known it completed by a quarter to twelve. I receive the meat and bread at the provision stores.

The port wine, and spirits, and arrowroot have been, until three days ago, issued in bulk to the surgery. Now, the man who issued them to the order-lies in the surgery issues them as assistant of the steward. The wine remains in the provision store. The steward opens the cases in presence of myself or a clerk. The assistant gives out the totals to the order-lies, and the orderlies sub-divide it again among the patients. I have no measures for dealing out, and have never had a requisition for any. The steward keeps books which I inspect at least half a dozen times a day.

It was not until four days ago that any complaint was made to me, that there were no means of boiling sago for the patients. I immediately sent a requisition to the barrack master for six Turkish braziers, and sent to the Commissariat for charcoal. I ordered that a cook should be told off for the purpose of cooking these extras. I think the Turkish braziers work well. I go in constantly to prevent waste of charcoal.

The delay in issuing meat for dinner arises from the steward having to issue to the orderlies of each ward in detail. I think it would be better if he were to issue to the assistant ward master, and let the ward-master sub-divide among the several messes.

There is great delay in issuing extras; I would dis-tribute the extras in the same way.

I regularly inspect all the privies almost every day. A party of fourteen native scavengers is employed for keeping them clean: a sergeant sees they do their duty. They go round three or four times a day. I have placed a washing tub in each place with Sir William Burnett's solution of chloride of zinc; I found, how-ever, that the patients were in the habit of emptying them and employing the tubs for washing their shirts, so I placed another tub there that they might use that. They now use both.

There is a great difficulty about returning the men their own shirts, but that arises from their not being marked. If they were marked with the men's names they would be returned to them. Each wardmaster could pick those of his men out of the whole number.

The clothing-pack and other property of the patient upon his admission are put up together, ticketed with his name and regiment, and sent down to the pack-store, where it is received by the sergeant in charge. I have never given any directions about opening the pack, and I believe it is not opened. I have never been applied to by any patient or by any other person to open the pack, or for leave to give out anything in the interior of the knapsacks. An application has been made to me for coatees, great coats, and boots for men going to Malta or home, and who had lost their own things. I gave orders they should be completed from the effects of dead men. We have no store for the supply of necessaries to the men. I have sometimes had applications from men returning to their duty, and I have supplied them in the same manner. When the dead men's effects do not supply the requisite articles, the applicant must be supplied from some other source. After I was last examined, orders were given to search the packs for shirts, and the return I sent you showed how few there were.

When I run short of any supplies, I report to Mr. Ward, except as to the things drawn from the commissariat. In that case I draw on commissariat. Since I have been in charge I have never been in want of medical comforts. I may have sometimes not had port until late in that day, but that is all. Deficiency of fowls only within the last two or three days. I spoke to Dr. Cruikshank the senior medical officer in Barrack hospital about it. Dr. Cruikshank said he would speak to the officers about it.

When a requisition cannot be complied with, the steward tells me. I have not heard lately of any want of essence of beef. I think we were without for two days sometime ago. The steward also sends word by the orderly to the medical officer that the article is not in store. The extras are drawn between three and four o'clock on that day. I have never heard of milk being wanting.

I have sometimes been unable to comply with requisitions for articles of hospital furniture, arising from not having any in store—bedsteads, urinals, close-stools, pans, and other matters of that kind. The "Triton" brought a supply of bedding lately from Varna. When I cannot comply, I draw my pen through the article in the requisition, and send word that I am unable to comply, but will do so when I receive a supply. When I cannot supply any of the articles, I return the requisition.

When things arrive, I send word generally to the medical officers that things have arrived in store, but I do not issue them without a fresh requisition. I keep no memorandum of the requisition I do not comply with.

I am in charge with a purveyor's clerk. He is quite young—about seventeen. He admitted to me that he never knew how to mend a pen until the last two days. That was the only assistance I had in the way of a clerk. I made frequent representations on this subject to Mr. Wreford. I did not get any further assistance until three days ago. I took charge November 1st. There were then two clerks, but they were engaged in bringing up arrears. One of them left for the Crimea towards the end of the month. Three days ago I received two non-commissioned officers. One of them, the more useful of the two, reported himself sick yesterday, because I had had occasion several times to check him for leaving the office. The non-commissioned officers are untrained men, and require my constant superintendence. I do not think I could get on without two efficient clerks, better than the young man I have. The average number of patients is between 1,800, and 1,900.

LIEUTENANT GORDON, Royal Engineers.
December 22nd

In charge of both hospitals since July. The General Hospital, generally speaking, is in good repair. The part used as a pack-store is in a very bad, almost dangerous condition—that is, the flooring of it. The kitchen also is in a bad state. The defect of that hospital is the want of water in the upper part of the building; it has to be forced up, and this is very often neglected by the Turks, whose duty it is to do it, and the patients have to carry it up themselves.

As to the kitchen, I have known, ever since I have been here, that it was in a bad state of repair. No application was made to me to have it put in repair, but an application was made to have the boilers reset, which I did. Two or three days ago I went there, and heard complaints from the cooks of the smoke. The purveyor (Mr. Ward) was present. I observed that no application had been made to me about the smoking of the kitchen, and he said he would send me a requisition. There is a great chimney in the kitchen, but it only begins at the top, and the smoke consequently escapes into the kitchen. It is very dark; it requires reflooring, and a proper chimney, and a place for baking and roasting would be very desirable. There would be no great difficulty in doing this. A kitchen is in course of construction for the officers. There is a capital Turkish bath room, but it is used as a necessary and urinal.

Two wings and a half of the Barrack hospital were in good repair when I took charge; the remainder was very much out of repair, scarcely habitable. I was required on the 9th November to repair the corridors and wards in the upper story in the old part of the building, comprising a wing and a half. I asked for materials. Lady Stratford directed me to give her a list of what I wanted. I did so. After a week's delay I got the necessary materials. I got a number of carpenters, masons, painters, and labourers, amounting to 150 at first, to 200 at present, and I have already put into repair 15 wards and one of the two corridors. They are fit for habitation and are now occupied. I am going on with the remainder, and should have had it all done if I had not been thrown over a dozen times by the contractor who supplies the materials. He is a Greek. It was an undecided question whether the Turkish or English governments were to pay for these works.

I received all my instructions about executing them from Lady Stratford on behalf of the Ambassador, but I did not act without a written authority from the Commandant, such as:

"Required to be repaired the floors, sashes, and flagstones in letters C. and D. corridors and rooms in the old parts of the barrack for hospital purposes.
Approved,
(Signed)
C. M. SILLERY, Major and Com."

The kitchen now in operation is very good as a barrack kitchen. The ventilation might be easily improved for carrying away steam that escapes into the apartment. I have had no application made to me for making in that kitchen an oven or a hot hearth or anything else for cooking extras; but I have made a kitchen near Miss Nightingale's quarters for the nurses for the use of the patients.

I have made one for sick officers. I am making another on one of the landings, and I am told I am to make another as soon as the works which I have now on hand are completed. The second branch kitchen is still unfinished. I applied personally to the commandant more than a month ago to have it made over to me in order to complete it. This was not done. I had no requisition made to me on the subject. The night before last, Lady Stratford, on behalf of the Ambassador, wrote to me that I was to put the kitchens into repair. I went to Lord Wm. Paulet and requested him to write to the Seraskier for the necessary coppers. I saw him write a letter accordingly but I have not heard of any answer.

I am about to put up some ventilators in the corridors to improve the ventilation.

The privies at the General Hospital are situated at the four external angles of the building, and are not as much complained of as those at the Barrack, which are placed in the inner angles. If they were properly sluiced out two or three times a day with water, and the soldiers did not throw bones and pieces of clothing down the pipes, the nuisance would be in a great measure obviated. The nuisance arises partly from the habits of the men.

Two of the corridors of the Barrack are 220 yards long, and each of the other two 194 yards each.

∞◦◦⊗◦◦∞

From the evidence given by Miss Florence Nightingale and one of her nurses, Miss Elizabeth Wheeler.

MISS FLORENCE NIGHTINGALE
December 23rd

I came on November 4th, with 38 nurses under my charge, for the purpose of nursing the sick and wounded soldiers in the hospitals at Scutari. I distributed them into wards. I gave Miss Wheeler four wards and a corridor (C) on the 8th Nov. I did not give any other nurse four wards.

She had only certain cases, 26 in number at first, to attend to, not to all the men in the wards. She came to me about the 10th, and told me Dr. M'Grigor had ordered negus for those cases that had been put down on her list. Dr. M'Grigor and I went round. I wrote the names of the men whom she was to attend. I sent for her and she made a copy from my list. She asked for negus when she told me it had been ordered. I gave it to her. She said she would require four bottles a day. I think that was about the third day after the negus had been first ordered. Before that, she did not ask for any specific quantity. She frequently remonstrated about not having enough port wine and rice pudding; afterwards also, about not having enough milk. In consequence of these remonstrances, I went, on one occasion, round the wards, examined the diet rolls, and saw what extras were ordered for the men. I stated to her I had reason to believe that the men obtained a double allowance of wine; that the orderlies drank the overplus; and that, therefore, it would be better if she brought the wine ordered by the medical men for the patients, and had it mulled in my kitchen. That was done. I have seen the orderlies drink the port ordered for the patients.

I inspected every day the wards under Miss Wheeler's charge. I turned my attention to the cases she had to attend. I do not think any of the men ever suffered for the want of port negus or any other thing. I think the supply given to them was quite sufficient. I think they suffered from taking the wine all at once. I have known a patient drink four gills at a draught. I think they also suffered from bad cookery; and the way a nurse can be chiefly useful, as I have repeatedly told Miss Wheeler, is by having the men's fowls brought here to be properly made into chicken broth, and by regulating the times and quantities at which the medical allowance is put into the men's mouths. I think that has been constantly neglected, as in the case of the man who drank the four gills at once, and remained without any wine for 24 hours. I have never had any report made to me by any of the nurses, or by any other person, that any life was ever lost in the hospital from the want of any restoratives or anything else being at hand. I do not think that any such case could have happened without its coming to my knowledge. It would have been the duty of any nurse seeing any case of emergency requiring restoratives, to apply to me at once at any time of the night. Miss Wheeler's wards are about 240 yards from my apartments.

No nurses have ever sat up during the night. They are not to be in the wards after half-past eight. They have sometimes rushed out against orders. In some special cases I have been called up during the night, when I have taken with me a nurse to attend to those cases. There are only three persons I ever employ in those cases. Miss Wheeler is not one. The nurses report to me every day the number of deaths in the wards which they attend. I am quite sure none ever reported to me as many as 11 deaths—five is the extreme number ever reported to me by any nurse. Miss Wheeler and other nurses have reported as large a number. The cases assigned to Miss Wheeler were very bad cases, but not by any means hopeless.

Within a few days after Miss Wheeler took charge of the wards, I directed that she should go round with the medical officer in the morning, and asked that officer, with Dr. M'Grigor's permission, to make an extra diet roll upon me. This was done. This was always attended to except twice, to the best of my recollection. The two occasions when it was not complied with were: first, when the milk turned, and it was impossible to supply milk that day; the other, when the requisition was for 80 rice puddings, 80 eggs, 80 half-pints of milk, 50 chicken broths. This requisition was brought to me at $12\frac{1}{2}$o'clock, p.m. The things were intended for the men's dinners at 1 o'clock, p.m. I had not time to prepare the things in so short a time. I gave all the rice puddings I had, and made extempore rice puddings of rice, cinnamon, and eggs.

Miss Wheeler never had any surgical cases to attend except one. She referred the case to me. I dressed the wound, reported the case to Dr. M'Grigor, and the man was moved the same afternoon.

The nurses are all distributed into wards. The medical men in charge of wards apply to me when they want nurses. I refer the application to the first class staff surgeon of the division, and with his permission. I send a nurse or nurses, of whom I have the selection. The general nature of their duties they learn from my orders. The patients to whom they are to attend are indicated to them by the medical officer; also the treatment of those patients. They are employed chiefly among the wounded, the operation cases, and the severe medical cases. Their duties among the surgical cases are, to go round in the morning, to wash and prepare such wounds for the medical officers as those officers direct, to attend the medical officers in their dressings, and receive and bring to me those officers' directions as to the diets, drinks, and medical comforts of those cases. They generally go out in fours. A quartet had generally a corridor and two wards of surgical cases. In the medical divisions the nurse's or nurses' duty is to take such cases as the medical officer confides to her. Her business is chiefly to see that the food is properly cooked and properly administered, that the extra diet rolls made on me are attended to, and that cleanliness, as far as possible, of the wards and persons is attended to, and bed sores dressed.

I have sometimes dressed wounds in the hospital. I have found maggots in several cases. I recollect at this moment two cases that I can mention. One was of a private (Smith) in ward 4, corridor B—an amputated thigh, and the wound sloughed. The case was regularly dressed twice a day. The evening before his death I assisted in dressing his wound. I picked out five or six maggots. The dressing had been performed carefully by Dr. Holton. The other case was a compound fracture of both bones of the leg, in ward 2, corridor A. I forget the man's name. The wound was carefully dressed twice and sometimes three times a day, by Mrs. Roberts, a nurse, who was for 23 years at St. Thomas's Hospital. I have seen her dress the wound, and assisted her; it was most carefully done. I found maggots within six hours after a dressing. The man is alive and doing well, likely to recover, and with his limb saved. I have seen her two hours dressing that wound. Not six hours after, I have taken maggots out.

February 20th

The articles I supplied—as shown in the list I have furnished to the commissioners—I supplied on the demands of medical officers in charge of wards, countersigned by staff surgeons of divisions.

Before complying with such requisition, I always inquired of the purveyor whether there were in his store any of the articles demanded. If he answered that there were none, then in most instances I went to the purveyor and asked him whether he expected any from England, or was about to get them from Stamboul. I went sometimes to the purveyor-in-chief, Mr. Wreford, sometimes to Mr. Stuart. Upon getting a negative answer, I issued them, if I had them in my store, or procured them in Stamboul. If the things were in the purveyor's store, I obtained them from him upon written requisition. The articles so obtained are shown on the list.

I have had my washing establishment since the 30th November. I employ from four to twelve soldiers' wives and widows there. They wash soldiers' shirts (flannel and cotton), socks, a few sheets, bandages, and drawers. On the 9th November we received the wounded after Inkerman. They were without shirts. I issued about 500. Before doing this I inquired of the purveyor whether he could supply them, and he said he could not. The purveyor was Mr. Wreford. This led to my finding out that other men who had been in hospital previous to Inkerman were without shirts, and I supplied about 700 more. This was during the first week. At the end of the first week the men informed me, that they still had the same shirts on. I inquired of Mr. Stuart, and found there was a contractor and a place for washing shirts. I did not interfere further for some days. At the end of that time I went with Mr. Bracebridge to Mr. Stuart, who told me the man had broken his contract, but that he was about to come to some fresh arrangement.

He erected a barrier, and ordered a sergeant to collect the shirts within it. Whether the shirts were collected or not, I do not know; but at the end of a fortnight, I, still finding the men were without change, went to him again. He told me that the contract had fallen through, and he gave the order that the shirts should be collected and distributed among four soldiers' wives. On the 20th day after Inkerman, a great number of those who had got shirts on the 9th, were still with the same shirts on their back. I inferred that the four soldiers' wives were not sufficient for washing the shirts, and I took a house at Scutari, provided it with boilers, which I obtained, partly from the engineer officers, partly from my own resources, and employed some soldiers' wives to wash.

I gave notice to the staff surgeons, that there was such an establishment, if they chose to have their patients' shirts washed. I was told by the non-commissioned officers that the men had been unwilling to give up their shirts to be washed either by the contractor, or by the soldiers' wives, because, they said, they either did not get back any shirts at all, or they got a bad one in place of a good one.

I also found that the washing of the soldiers' wives was quite insufficient. They washed in a tub, generally in cold water; and it is necessary that shirts in hospital should be boiled, because it is impossible to get out, otherwise, the animal matter. This is particularly detrimental, when A gets B's shirt. I believe the surgeons of divisions ordered their wardmasters to collect the dirty shirts, and to send them to my establishment. I made a fresh issue of shirts, in order to enable them to comply. The number washed has varied, from 50 to 800. I was struck with this, and on inquiry, I was told by a wardmaster, that the purveyor had told him to take the shirts to the soldiers' wives.

It appeared to be optional with the wardmaster, whether he should obey the surgeon or the purveyor. I have now, from 500 to 800 pieces a week. I think the shirts come, generally, from the same quarter. Each wardmaster delivers up his shirts to me, and I give him a receipt. I do my best to ensure the return of the identical shirts. I direct that the shirts of each wardmaster shall be washed in a separate tub. I obtained the tubs from the purveyor. The men are not, now, properly supplied with clean shirts. There are several reasons for that. I have patients, at this moment, without shirts. The number of those wholly without shirts does not exceed ten; but there is not a sufficient supply for the hospital.

The men who come from the Crimea are in such a state of filth, that the shirts have to be cut off from them; and when they leave the hospital, they are allowed to take away the shirts on their backs. I could not refuse it. Another reason for the insufficiency of clean shirts is that the soldiers' wives employed by the purveyor have no means of procuring hot water, or other conveniences, for washing. I have heard of a woman giving a man a pint of porter, to get her some hot water. In my establishment, I could do any amount of washing; but, in this climate, we cannot dry without wringing machines. These I expect daily from England.

I have observed how the bedding which is washed by contract is washed. The blankets come back torn and covered with stains. I have, myself, sorted these blankets when taking in sick, and been compelled to throw away the so-called clean blankets, till they could be carried away and destroyed. They also come so wet, that I am obliged to have them dried before they can be used.

With respect to the articles in the lists which are properly apothecaries' stores, I applied to the apothecary before issuing them. I put the same questions as I did to the purveyor. As for stump pillows, I got from him oil cloth enough to make about two dozen. The medical officers complained that the quality was bad, that the oil was decomposed by the discharge from the wounds of the patients.

As to medical comforts, the beef we have always had from the purveyor. The chickens were sometimes so bad that I have often had to return them to the purveyor. He said he could get no better. Our cook could not make soup with them; so, to make soup, I was obliged to get others. Arrowroot has been supplied to me in part by the purveyor. Only on one occasion did he give me half the quantity I asked for; on the others, he always gave me the quantity I asked, but our own arrowroot was much better. For the sick it is important to have the best. The sago I asked for of the purveyors, but did not get. The lemons also they declined giving me. The milk was so bad that I could not use it for sick cookery, and I could not get enough; so I always supplied it myself.

The port wine was declined. The medical officers came to me from different divisions, and said the port wine was bad, and asked me for some. This has frequently happened. The same with the brandy. Brandy was never refused to us, but it was bad. The medical officers asked me for it. The eggs I used to get from the purveyor. About two months ago my requisitions for them began to be refused. When my requisitions had been declined a number of times, I ceased to apply, and have ever since supplied the eggs from private sources. They have been very scarce, and very dear during that period; so has milk, so have chickens.

With regard to the wine, I used to issue arrowroot without wine, even after the medical officers made requisitions on me, and I insisted on the men putting into it the port which they got from the purveyor. I did not issue the wine, until the medical officers said the port was so bad.

MISS ELIZABETH WHEELER, one of the nurses of the Scutari Hospital, under Miss Nightingale. *December 22nd*

Came here on 5th November. Four wards and a corridor (now C corridor) were assigned to me. My duties were to watch the men and carry relief in the shape of extras. These were anything that could be procured. Miss Nightingale told me that if I wanted anything, I should apply to her. I entered on my duties on the 8th or 9th. I went round first in the forenoon with Miss Nightingale and Dr. McGrigor. I commenced that day, and was in constant attendance on the men. The wards contained the worst cases of diarrhœa, dysentery, fever, and diseases of the chest. I have since had reason to believe that they were hopeless cases. I had to supply them with wine. Dr. McGrigor ordered that the men should have any restoratives that I could devise. In consequence of that order, I desired to give wine to about 50—port wine negus. Dr. McGrigor's order was not given until two or three days after we had first gone round.

The first order Dr. McGrigor gave was when I went round with him and Miss Nightingale. Dr. D'Arcey, the assistant surgeon in charge of the wards, was present. It was then he spoke about the restoratives generally. I never saw Dr. D'Arcey with a diet roll in his hand. I seldom saw him in the wards. I think his morning visits had been paid before I went to the wards. I used to go from nine till ten, and I was there for the rest of the day backwards and forwards. It was two or three days after, that Dr. McGrigor ordered hot negus. He said, in one of the wards, "These men should have hot wine, or negus." I made a mistake in saying there were only four wards; there were seven, two little ones containing from 12 to 14 men, and five large ones containing more than thirty each. The first day I gave them restoratives— egg-wine, arrowroot, chicken, chicken broth, and beef tea. I got these things at Miss Nightingale's quarters. Afterwards I got them in the same way. There was a difficulty in getting them, but I always got them. When I wanted anything I called at Miss Nightingale's quarters personally. I always saw either Miss Nightingale or Mrs. Bracebridge. I asked them for what I wanted. I did not get as much as I wanted or said I wanted. This was general. I always thought the men would have been better if I could have taken it to them. I never had any communication with Dr. D'Arcey on the subject of giving the men the things.

I have had a great deal of experience in attending the sick before I came here, for the last six years especially. I had a good deal of that work in 1849, in the cholera, at Plymouth. I used to go to both hospitals, night and day. I had sufficient experience to be able to judge about the quantities to give the men.

The want of the things I found mostly at the beginning. It was my impression that the men suffered from the want. I think all the men I had to attend to were in a state of great exhaustion. I think that perhaps 50 men may have had their healths injured by the want of the restoratives I desired to give them. This was especially within the first few days. I never made any representation to Dr. D'Arcey on the subject. I did not mention it to Dr. McGrigor. I mentioned it to Miss Nightingale. I was continually in communication with her. I do not recollect any particular occasion. I never was in the wards during their regular meals. The men used to tell me they never got anything except what I brought them—except tea, which they did not like. Several of them had wine allowed by the doctor—generally two gills a day. Some had brandy.

When Dr. McGrigor ordered the port negus, I got some at once from Miss Nightingale. I do not recollect whether she gave me enough; I always found it short from the first. I then made a written requisition on Miss Nightingale, specifying the quantity required. For a short time I got the quantity.

Most of the cases died.

Dr. McGrigor then said he did not think stimulants saved those who were most far gone, but I think that some were decidedly brought round by it. Each man got half a pint of negus. I gave them near upon that quantity. When I was short of it, I gave it to the worst cases—that is, to those who needed it most, and those who were the most exhausted. The others, on those occasions, went without any port negus. The first day I gave negus to only about 12 men. I gradually increased the number up to 80. When I was short of negus, I made it up with an egg beat up in about a tablespoonful of port, or Marsala, or brandy. I considered that was a satisfactory substitute. I think there was little difference between them, but I do not think anything I gave them affected their health, wine more than the other. But they liked the negus best, and I therefore gave it to them. I used to make, from the first day, a list of those whom I thought fit objects for the negus. I put down the names of some men in the presence of Miss Nightingale and Dr. McGrigor, when I got the list, on the first day. I did not add any more without submitting their names to the doctor.

I had no occasion to consult Dr. D'Arcey, for I made no addition while he remained in charge. After him came Dr. Maclise. I never saw him. Then the wards were divided into two. Mr. Hollingsworth and Mr. Maclean were the two surgeons. I used to see them constantly. I used to speak to them on the subject of giving the men wine and other nourishment. Dr. Maclean preferred milk and eggs. After Dr. McGrigor said he did not think the stimulants did the good he expected of them, the supply was restricted altogether. We used to heat the wine, which was issued to the men from the stores.

I would have given negus to a great many more than those on my list, if there had been a larger supply. I would have given to all. It would have done harm to none of them. There were no men in fever. Some had had fever.

I think there was a want of good chickens. The extras ordered by the doctors were in general supplied. Milk and eggs were often not supplied. This went on until the wards were broken up, about a fortnight ago. I think the health of the men suffered from the want of milk and eggs. I recollect many instances when men would not take what they did not like; and milk was an especial treat. When milk was short, I used to give them arrow-root or chicken-broth, or something else. This did not please them as well, and I think their health might have been injured in consequence. I found the medical men attended to the patients carefully in prescribing the diets and extras.

After the first few days, I used to get four bottles of port daily. I would have given to a larger number if I had had the supply. I did not say that to the doctors; I think I did to Miss Nightingale.

I cannot say that there was a single case in which a man lost his life from the want of port wine, or any other thing. The men died very fast. Many were in a dying state when I went to them, and I do not think that restoratives would have revived any of those who did die. I do not recollect a single case where I was unable to get restoratives in any emergency. The daily mortality in my wards was four, five, or six. I do not think it ever exceeded six; I do not recollect that it ever amounted to six.

From the evidence given by other individuals at the Barrack hospital, Scutari.

The Rev. J. E. SABIN
December 14th

I have been here since last July. I was present when the first wounded arrived. I think it was on Sunday, but we had a large batch of sick on Friday. There was a great want in the Barrack hospital of bedsteads and beds. The sick and wounded were put into the wards; some, not all, had beds, many without them. When the wounded arrived, they all had to lie on the floor. Corridors B and C were filled with men lying down, some had straw beds, but the majority were without anything under them, some without even a coat. I recollect the circumstance; because on the Monday morning at 3 a.m., I assisted Dr. McGrigor in distributing the blankets, and we found some poor fellows without even a coat. Some had got hold of beds, but they were very few. The surgeons attended to them as fast as they could, but it was impossible to attend to them all. The surgeons were up, I believe, all night. I observed them dressing the wounds. I did not observe, myself, whether there was lint and the other surgical appliances, but I presume there was, because I saw the surgeons hard at work, and heard no complaints of any want. The complaint was that they could not apply the dressings fast enough.

I was in every corner of the hospital every day. Whenever I was called to a dying man, I went. Besides, I was seeking for them. During all that time I never a heard a complaint of the want of any surgical appliances or medicines from the surgeons, but I did hear complaints from the men that they did not get their medicines. Several men told me that they had not been dressed for several days. Three days is the longest time I heard. One of the men was a sergeant in the Scots Fusilier Guards. He was in the General Hospital, and he walked up here three or four days after. He is now gone home.

At the General Hospital things were very bad on the same Sunday. When I left the hospital at about

11 p.m., there must have been from 200 to 300 men choking up the passages and stair-case near the chief entrance. The surgeons were examining them and sending them to bed as fast as they could. There were a great number of beds. I should say there must have been beds for nearly all—not all, for I found some next morning lying upon the stones, covered with their coats. In the course of a week's time, at any rate, every man must have had a bed in both hospitals, I should say.

The complaints I heard among the men for the first seven or eight days, were chiefly of want of surgical attendance and want of regular food. They got their food at long intervals and irregularly. I speak now chiefly of this hospital. At the other hospital the same complaints were made by the officers. They complained that the surgeons came late, not that they did not come at all. The cooking was universally condemned. I never saw a case of wilful neglect. I saw a statement in a paper from a clergyman, who said that his brother had been here for a fortnight without even seeing a surgeon. I can only say that I always found the surgeons perfectly ready at all times. When it is recollected that this enormous building was filled in a week, and what the staff was, the only wonder is, that things were not worse.

EDWARD JENNINGS, Private in 88th Regt.
December 14th

Arrived at the General Hospital September 22nd. I was sick. I got up the day the wounded came from

Alma, to see if there were any wounded of my own regiment there. Some of them lay in the corridors without beds that night. The most part were in beds; the rest got beds the next day. They seemed to have their bedding all right. I cannot say about sheets; I had sheets to my own bed. The surgeons were very busy bandaging up wounds. I did not hear any of the surgeons or any body else complain of not having what they wanted for dressing wounds; but I heard the men complaining along the passages as I went in, that their wounds were not washed and dressed. That was the first night they came in. I did not hear any more complaints of the kind next day, nor any time afterwards. While the men were complaining, the surgeons were working at the other side of the hospital.

I have been an orderly ever since September 29th. I commence at about $6\frac{1}{2}$ a.m.; go to the purveyor's store and get the bread. I have the diet roll with me. The steward deals out the bread. The orderlies fall in in order as they come down, and are served in that way. There are nearly 200 orderlies in it. It takes an hour and a half to serve it out. I get whole loaves, and then I cut it up. Either I or the other orderly goes for the tea; we do not have to wait more than 20 minutes. I never have breakfast in my ward later than 8 o'clock.

At 9 I go and draw the meat. I get it, also, from the steward; he has bread, meat, and salt to serve out together, and sometimes he has not done till near 1 o'clock. I do not take the diet roll with me because the steward in the morning enters in a large book the quantity marked on the diet roll with the name of the orderly who is to get it. I generally get my dinner by 2 o'clock.

As soon as I get the diet roll, that is, as soon as the doctor has done with it, I go to the steward again. As soon as he has done serving out the ordinary rations, he serves the officers' servants, and then he serves us our extras—mutton chops, extra bread, chickens, porter, lemons, and eggs. I serve out the porter, and then I go down again to get my wine, arrowroot, sugar, sago, beef tea, brandy, or anything else. This I get at the same place from the corporal, who gets the things from the purveyor. If the dinner is early, I serve it out before I get the extras; if late, I draw the extras first. I have them there until the dinners are over, and then I go and cook the extras. I have always done this since I have been an orderly. I don't boil the chickens in the kitchen copper as most do, because I could not cook it there till the following day, and I like to give the men their dinners without there being any grumbling. I boil them in an old tin belonging to a man in the ward, who does not care about it. I also cook the sago and other things as well as I can. I cook them either in the cook-house, or in the shed near the post-office.

The diet roll does say at what times the extras are to be taken; the doctor does not give me any directions. I cook all the extras and give them at once to the man, and he can then do what he likes with them. I generally get 2 oz. of arrowroot for each man. If he does not eat it all he gives it to his neighbours.

I never was an orderly until I was sent into this ward. I did not like to go as orderly, but the adjutant picked me out of the ranks with others as the strongest men.

Except taking my regular turn of duty to cook for my company, I never did anything in the way of cooking until I became an orderly.

During their work the Parliamentary Commissioners found the state of the Barrack hospital to be so awful and so dangerous, that they appointed an Inspector of Nuisances. This gentleman reported as follows.

Report by MR. JAMES WILSON, Inspector of Nuisances at Scutari Hospitals.

Scutari

In accordance with my instructions, I beg to report that on 17th March, I commenced operations at the Barrack hospital with 13 men. During the day outside of the hospital and one fourth of the hospital square were swept, and 13 handcarts of filth and offensive matter removed; nine dead dogs lying in the vicinity of the hospital were buried. The flushing apparatus for the privies and sewers could not be used, as the workmen had not finished them.

March 19th Thirteen men employed, who swept the barrack square, the ground outside the hospital and the adjacent streets of the village. A large pit was dug in the field near the Turkish burying ground, and the carcasses of four dogs and two horses placed therein; 19 handcarts of filth and rubbish were removed from the privies and from the hospital precincts and 12 large baskets of filth from the adjacent streets.

March 20th Thirteen men employed, who swept the ground surrounding the hospital, the barrack square, and the streets adjacent; 20 handcarts of filth and rubbish from the privies, and from the places swept, removed to the appointed place of deposit; I made use of peat charcoal before removing the offensive matter from the privies. Fourteen baskets of filth removed from the streets in the village, and two dead dogs buried.

March 21st Thirteen men employed on the same work as yesterday, and peat charcoal again used. Nineteen hand-carts of filth and rubbish were taken from the privies and the vicinity of the hospital, and twelve large baskets full from the streets near it.

March 22nd Thirteen men similarly employed. Twenty-five handcarts of filth and rubbish were taken from the privies and the vicinity of the hospital and eight large baskets full from the streets; peat and charcoal was again used before removing the offensive matter from the privies.

March 23rd Thirteen men similarly employed. I had two of the privies which had been lately repaired cleaned out, and deodorised with peat charcoal; 26 handcarts of filth and rubbish were removed from the streets and hospital.

The water closet attached to Lord William Paulet's quarters being in an offensive state, I cleaned it out myself and applied peat charcoal.

March 24th Fifteen men employed at the Barrack and five at the General Hospital, who swept the barrack squares and the places adjoining; 24 handcarts of filth and rubbish were removed from the Barrack and ten from the General Hospital.

The flushing apparatus on the west side of the Barrack hospital being this day completed, I used them with the best effect; I employed four men to fill the tanks, and emptied them three times during the day.

I beg further to state that I find it very difficult to get the men to work.

PART 5

∞⋙⋘∞

The Select Committee of the House of Commons Enquiry into the War in the Crimea. Evidence given in London in March 1855.

∞⊗∞

THE HONOURABLE SIDNEY GODOLPHIN OSBORNE

What was your position at Scutari?

I simply went out on my own account, unconnected with any office or with anybody, but sanctioned by the Secretary-at-War, Mr. Sidney Herbert; but the first day I got there I volunteered my services to assist Mr. Sabin, the head chaplain and I for a certain time took charge of a part of the hospital in which the cholera and dysentery wards were.

In what state did you find the hospitals?
Nothing could be worse. The Barrack hospital was in a disgraceful state. I cannot consider it was a hospital in the state in which I found it; there was no apparent system, and certainly very little of what I should call the order of an hospital.

Did you find any want of medicines in the hospital?
With regard to the medicines, the first time that the want was called to my attention was on the Sunday after I got there. I had an accident with Sir Edward Colebrook, which ended in our both going into the Bosphorous, on my way to do duty there, and I had to sleep in the hospital that night; it was impossible to return, and I dined with the chaplain. He was taken ill at dinner with an attack of a mild sort of cholera; I found him in the surgeon's, Dr. McGregor's, room, and it was proposed to give him the simplest possible draughts in a case of that sort, and the dispenser was sent for. I saw him at the door, and I heard him tell Dr. McGregor that there was no confectio opii in the dispensary at all.

Can you give the committee any notion of the wants of articles in the hospital?
With regard to linen I can state at once that I was present when, at Miss Nightingale's request, Mr. Macdonald wrote an advertisement to be put in "The Times" newspaper with a request that linen should be sent out to Scutari.

Were you able to find any head in the hospital?
Never, nor in Constantinople at all. I have frequently said that the two things I wished most to find when I was offered many relics for a museum, for my family, were the truth and a head with responsibility, but I found neither.

What was your opinion of the discipline in the hospital?
Where there is no head I can hardly say I could expect discipline. Here the committee must understand it is difficult to make people in England understand the size of the hospital and the nature of the proceedings for bringing the sick from ships to it. To keep up discipline would require a perfect system.

There appears to have been, also, a determination, not avowed, but too evident, for "the honour of the service" to conceal the real state of things, and to trust to the speedy arrival of stores and officers said to be on their way, and also to the hope that the battle of the Alma would end such sudden demands on resources at Scutari.

The stores published as having been sent from England, may have been so sent, but if this is the case I can only say, I cannot discover where they possibly can have been lost, consumed they have not been; should the truth ever appear in the matter, did it once burst the bounds of official fear, you would I think discover that there has been grave misconduct; otherwise the government could not have been so deceived, the service so wronged.

Nothing could be more dreadful than the dysentery and cholera wards. They were in the only part of the hospital that was not burnt down some years ago; it was the oldest part; there were no bedsteads. The thin stuffed sacking that they laid upon floors, perfectly rotten and full of vermin; and as I have kneeled by the side of the men, they crawled over my hand onto my book; in fact the place was alive with them. I have asked the orderlies why were those floors not cleaned; and the answer was, and Dr. McGregor told me so, that the wood was so rotten, that if it were properly washed it could not be got dry again. I complained so repeatedly of the condition of those poor creatures, to whom my duty took me every day, that at last they were moved, and spread about for a time amongst the other patients; and then they set about to repair a large new ward.

The engineer, a most active young gentleman of the name of Gordon, came one morning and told me that 60 Turks — I think as many as that — had struck and refused work, unless they were told who was to pay them. Miss Nightingale at once offered to become responsible for all sums of money necessary. I said to Mr. Gordon that must not be, and I should infinitely rather be answerable myself. I was afraid lest she should get into any trouble for interfering in a thing of that sort.

Do you remember any meat being served out raw?
I have seen it again and again. I have passed down the ward. You may call it dinner, if you like; but I have

seen meat brought up raw into the ward and put upon a board, and the orderly took a stick or a knife, and, with a list before him, cut it into rations. I called Dr. McGregor's attention to the meat being, I may say, absolutely raw. And poor man I do not know that he could do anything; there was not the means of properly cooking the meat.

Supposing "The Times" fund and yourself had not been there, in what state do you think the hospital would have been?
I must add one other element, namely, supposing Miss Nightingale and her nurses had not been there. In short if that aid, which I conceive no Government had a right to calculate upon, had not been there, I can conceive nothing more disastrous than the state of things which would have existed.

Did you ever hear what had become of, or any reason given for the absence of, all those stores which have been supplied in such great abundance from England?
I have never yet heard a reason which has at all satisfied me. My firm belief is, that the great majority of them never left England; and my still further belief is, that no ingenuity will ever discover them, unless it is put in a very different train of inquiry from any I have heard yet.

It would be a question for the police, you submit?
Undoubtedly. I will put it to the committee to take merely the tonnage which I have got here. There are

50,000 bottles of port wine bought in bulk. Will any gentleman here tell me that 50,000 bottles of port wine could be bought in the London wine market and not influence the London wine market; and can he produce any gentleman to say that the London wine market were affected.

You speak of 4,000 dozen of wine?
Four thousand and eighty dozen and that would be 50,000 bottles.

Are you aware that this committee has now returns before it showing that the quantity of port wine sent to the Crimea has been between 16,000 and 17,000 dozen?
My credulity has been so stretched that I can believe it.

Did you ever hear of convalescents being drunk with the port wine?
Never; I never saw but one drunken man and he had nothing to do with the hospital at all.

MR. JOHN MACDONALD of "The Times" newspaper.

*You went out, did you not, to administer the charitable fund
for "The Times"?*
Yes.

*"The Times," in consequence of certain reports from our troops
in Scutari, appealed to the charity of the British public to furnish them with the means of providing them with comforts?*
I believe so.

The British Government had the same opportunity, had they not, of administering to their wants as "The Times" had?

Much better I should say. They have, in the East, consular agents, they have an ambassador and they access an infinite command of money. The agent of "The Times" was not aware of the state of the markets; he knew nothing of the East before, and he had to squeeze out with considerable difficulty the secret of what was wanted in the hospitals.

Before you went out on this mission to distribute this charitable fund, had you any communication with any member of the government here?

I saw the Duke of Newcastle, the Minister for War, and I saw Dr. Andrew Smith, the Chief Medical Officer for the army.

Did you obtain from them any information with respect to the general state of the hospitals?

I was told that it was not likely that a fund of that sort would be found of any use in the relief of the sick and the wounded.

Do you know what the number of patients was in the respective hospitals and on board the hospital ships at the time of your arrival?

No, there were no returns of any kind prepared at that time; everything relating to the statistics of the medical establishments was more or less in a state of confusion; there were not even returns of deaths on board ship;

and the returns of the deaths in the hospitals were inaccurately given; as to a very large proportion of the deaths which took place in the army at that time, from sickness and from wounds, after leaving the Crimea, there remained no records; and the number of burials did not, almost to the last moment when I left, correspond with the number of deaths; even at Scutari the number returned of the deaths did not correspond with the actual number of burials.

In what state did you find the Barrack hospital?
In the Barrack hospital very small provision had been made for converting it into a hospital at all. The sick occupied a series of wards, the floor of which was in a very bad state; the flooring was open and rotten and they lay upon the boards in situations where they could not obtain the necessary warmth in the treatment of their complaints.

In what state was the ventilation of that hospital?
It became worse afterwards; as the number of dysenteric cases increased, the ventilation became exceedingly bad. The construction of the hospital is an open quadrangle, round which run a series of corridors, with wards and small rooms adjoining. The corridors were occupied by patients, as well as the wards and by double rows of patients, the result of which was that as the number of dysenteric patients increased, the emanations from them were carried into the wards of adjoining and into the rooms occupied by the surgeons and the officers.

The hospital was in a state which, from the infectious diseases of the air, admitted very little hope?
Very little.

Now applying yourself to one particular object, suppose there was a great want of shirts for the wounded and the sick, could they not have been supplied within 24 hours in Constantinople?
Yes.

When you were there, did Miss Nightingale arrive?
She arrived two days before my arrival.

Are you cognisant of any difficulties being placed in her way?
I should say so.

Of what nature?
I know, practically, that only one medical officer, having the control of a division, at first used much of her supplies, although those supplies could not be obtained from the purveying department.

So that the patients were in want, and near at hand there were the means of supply, which supply was not used by the persons in authority?
Yes, I know also that the patients whose cases obviously required nursing, had no nurses furnished to them by the medical officers whose duty it was to provide the nursing, with the exception of one medical officer.

So that nurses were offered by Miss Nightingale and not accepted by the medical officer?
I should say that the nurses were not used to the extent that they might have been in nursing the patients.

Amongst the comforts afforded by you was there port wine?
Yes.

Do you know the quality of the port wine supplied by the government?
I tasted it.

What was it like?
I tasted it, and I could detect logwood distinctly, and certainly brandy and a sort of vin ordinaire, not port wine.

Will you state the condition of the soldiers' wives?
Nothing can convey to the committee any idea of the spectacle presented by the manner in which the soldiers' wives lived at Scutari, and the rooms in which they lived.

In what way?
There was one small room in which there were at one time as many as 48 soldiers' wives, some of them with children, and others of them sleeping with their husbands there, in a state in which the worst lodging houses in the lowest and worst parts of the metropolis before the Lodging House Act presented a favourable comparison.

Was the atmosphere very pestiferous in that room?
I shall never forget it; you could not remain in there
five minutes without being sick.

*Was any attempt made to organize these women into any
kind of corps of nurses?*
I am afraid that it would have been impossible.

Why?
The effect of the war upon the character of the
women had been such, that any attempt to turn them
to useful account, I am afraid, would have failed.

*How many women at any time were there assembled
together in the Scutari barracks?*
There were nearly two hundred when I left.

They were sent out by the government, were they not?
They were permitted to go by a lamentable mistake.

*Were they under no superintendence; was there nobody to
look after them?*
There was no governmental superintendence. The
government appeared to deal with them in this
fashion: they appeared to permit them, and they
existed as best they could under the circumstances
of the hospital; most of them were living upon the
lowest floor of the hospital, under all the sickness,
and I remember particularly one room, which had
in its corner a leaky pipe, down which all the night
soil came.

Who was at the head at the time when you say the women were in that dreadful state?
During the period of four months the hospital had six changes of head.

On the subject of forms, will you illustrate by an example the mischief of forms?
I do not know that I could give a better illustration of the effect of forms than the case of an officer who died at Missirie's hotel, who was placed under arrest on the day of his death for non-compliance with forms, which his state of health rendered it impossible that he could attend to.

Will you describe the case?
It was that of Captain Williams, of the Scots Greys, an officer well known in the service. He had been in charge at Balaklava, and had eminently distinguished himself in the charge, but was taken ill with dysentery shortly afterwards; he was struck down by it and was in a state of extreme exhaustion; he was brought down to Balaklava, where he might have remained upon the pier, but for the attention of the postmaster, Mr Smith, who took him into his house. He was carried on board ship, utterly unable to comply with the forms, which are requisite for the removal of an officer; his life depended upon immediate removal. He was taken down to the Bosphorous, and in such a state of prostration, that it was more convenient and easy, under the circumstances, to have him taken to Missirie's hotel than over to the hospital; and because

he had not reported himself, or complied with the forms which were requisite, in some extraordinary way, a few hours before his death, he was arrested.

By military authority?
By military authority.

THE DUKE OF NEWCASTLE, Minister of War

When did you first determine to send out nurses the hospital?
It must have been about the middle of October I think; I really cannot say exactly.

What induced you to send them out?
The question of the employment of the nurses had been mooted at a very early stage (before in fact the

army left this country) and the general opinion of military men was adverse to their employment. It had been tried upon former occasions, and I believe the class of women that had been tried had been ordinary hospital nurses, and they had been found to be very much addicted to drink, and often more callous to the sufferings of the soldiers than those male attendants who had been employed more recently.

Under these circumstances, they were very adverse to it, but when we found the great complaints that were made and conveyed to me, not merely by the public press and by private letters, but by gentlemen who came over from Constantinople at the time, and who had recently visited the hospitals, we felt it to be our duty to take such steps as we could to remedy such a state of things and we reverted, amongst other things to the proposal of nurses.

The difficulty was to find any lady who was competent to undertake so great a task as the organisation of such a body; and I confess I despaired, having seen one or two, of making the attempt, until Mr. Sidney Herbert, then Secretary-at-War, being personally acquainted with Miss Nightingale, with whom I also had the honour of being acquainted, suggested that it might be possible to induce her to undertake so great a task, though we felt great delicacy in proposing it. We found, however, at once, she was willing, and we felt that anything she undertook would be successful.

Did you hear, except through the public newspapers, and through private channels, of the miseries suffered by our troops in the hospital and on the passage from Balaklava to Scutari?

I did not.

You had no official information on the suffering of the troops?

No.

When were you made acquainted with the state of things at Scutari and at Balaklava?

At the end of December.

Up to that time you had no official information of the real state of things?

No, I had not.

After that time were you informed officially of what had occurred?

Not in detail.

MR. P. B. MAXWELL, member of the Parliamentary Commission.

You were a member of the commission that was sent out by the government to inspect the state of the hospitals at Scutari?
Yes, I was.

During the time you were at Scutari what was the condition of the patients with respect to medical comforts; were they properly supplied?
I think in the main they were, with the assistance of

Miss Nightingale, the extent of whose assistance I can tell the committee. Finding I could not get from the purveyor the returns of information which we had demanded, the best way was to apply to Miss Nightingale. I knew that Miss Nightingale had established a kitchen almost immediately after her arrival at Scutari, chiefly for the purpose of cooking medical comforts, and I asked her if she could give me an account of the average supplies issued from that kitchen for the months of December and January. I asked her first for December, and she gave me a return for that month. I asked her whether, before issuing those goods, she had applied to the purveyor to ascertain whether the things were in store or not and Miss Nightingale said that she had in respect to some of the things, but with respect to the chicken broth, arrowroot, milk, port wine, brandy and chickens, she supplied them, not because they were not in store, but because the goods in the purveyor's store were not of good quality.

Including the port wine?
Yes, she told me that it had been represented to her by one of the surgeons that the port wine was very bad, that it was made of logwood, and that in consequence she issued fifteen bottles daily. I have no doubt that the gentleman who expressed his opinion upon the port wine was right as to what he tasted. I can only say that I tasted it once and I thought it was so good that I tasted it three or four times afterwards, and always about the middle of the day. I thought it

exceedingly good; but have no doubt there was a variety; and that there was good and bad, and that while the surgeon fell upon the bad I alighted upon the good.

The person who supplied you with port wine knew that you were a commissioner from the government did he not?
I did not give him time to inquire about it; I went down to the stores about the middle of the day, where I saw a man surrounded by port wine bottles, of which he was drawing the corks as fast as he could, dealing out the orderlies their gills of port. I stepped up to him and said, "Give me a glass of that." He did so, and I thought it very good. As I have said, I tried it on two or three occasions and liked it very much; if I may be permitted to add, I think it is better port wine than we get in the Temple. Moreover I wish to say, in my opinion Miss Nightingale's services have been invaluable to the hospital, but in a great measure in keeping the purveyors to their duty; if Miss Nightingale had not been there, the hospital would not have been nearly so well supplied.

⚬⟡⟡⟡⚬

DR. W. H. FLOWER

How many days were the greater part of those sick men on board "The Victoria" from the time they were put on board till the time they actually landed?
Ten or eleven days.

Do you know how many men died during that period?
Between 20 and 30; I forget the exact number.

As a medical man, do you think that that number would have died, supposing proper care had been taken of the sick

in providing necessaries, keeping them clean, and landing them at the proper time?
Some certainly would have died, for they were all in such a wretched state when they were put on board, but I should think not so many.

You attribute the deaths of a great many men to insufficient preparations; can you say how many?
It is impossible to say; I was sick myself and could not pay much attention to the sick.

Do you remember the order of Dr. Hall, with respect to chloroform being used in operations?
Yes, he stated that chloroform should not normally be used during amputation operations.

What impression did that order make?
The younger medical men, who had seen so much of the use of chloroform in the London hospitals, did not quite agree in the opinion given there certainly.

Notwithstanding that order, did you, and the surgeons in your division, use chloroform?
Yes, we always did.

Did you find any evil effects from the use of chloroform?
Not at all; I had seen it used a great deal in London, having been a house surgeon to a large London hospital before I joined the army, and certainly it was my opinion, that in almost all cases of amputations, chloroform should be given, not only through

motives of humanity, but as tending to the safety of the operation.

Did you use it in gun-shot wounds?
I had not seen much of gun shot wounds before, but we did use it there.

Did you ever lose a patient in consequence of the use of chloroform?
No, we did not at all.

DR. ANDREW SMITH, Director-General of the Army and Ordnance Medical Department.

Is it your view that the opinion of any of the civil surgeons of the London hospitals upon the propriety or not of administering chloroform before an operation is not worth much?
I should say, with reference to that question, that if any experienced and clever surgeon of a London hospital should tell me that he has seen a man fall from the top of a building in London, and have his thigh shattered from the hip joint, the leg and have the bone commuted and fractured into 100 pieces, or

the case of a man having an arm shot off or torn off, that he before performing his operations used chloroform and found it advantageous, then I should say his opinion was of value; but when I hear men say that chloroform ought to be used, I suspect that they do not take into consideration the exact condition into which soldiers are often brought by cannon shots, with life hardly existing, but where the medical officer can only say, "If I do nothing the man will die, therefore I had better risk and try to save his life," in such a case it would I think be perfectly out of the question to administer chloroform; it would kill him at once, the little life that remained would be perfectly extinguished.

My question had reference to the sneers that have been in the papers about the expression of Dr. Hall; and I want to know whether, in your opinion, Dr. Hall was right in thinking that it was not necessary at all times to use chloroform for amputations?
I think that Dr. Hall was perfectly right; but that as he might have known that it would be in opposition to a great number who have strong prejudices in favour of chloroform, it would have been better to have communicated private information to the different medical officers, instead of embodying that regulation in the general regulations which he issued.

Who was Dr. Hall and why was he appointed?
He was, in the first place, appointed because he happened to be the senior deputy inspector-general

in the service; a man of high professional acquire-
ments during five years in the Kafir war; of great
powers of observation, and of highly cultivated intel-
lect; a man who was universally respected and
esteemed by the whole army.

Was he appointed by you?
Yes.

Did he report to you upon the state of the hospital at Scutari?
He said, on his leaving in November, that the hospitals
were in as good a state as it could possibly be expected.

*Did you consider that report to be satisfactory, after what you
had seen elsewhere?*
I must trust to the officers of my own department,
who are responsible.

*Were not the terms of his order these, that it was better to
hear a man bawl under the knife than to see him sink under
the operation?*
I am not prepared to justify those words.

*You state that it was the duty of the medical officers to have
provided everything for the comfort and convenience of those
patients; can you tell the committee how you account for the
difference between the state of things as described and that
which you supposed to exist at the time of your conversation
with Mr. MacDonald?*
It is difficult for me to say.

Supposing that the bazaars at Constantinople could furnish the means of supplying those hospital dresses, they ought to have been obtained for the relief of the patients, ought they not?
Clearly.

Who do you suppose was responsible for not obtaining them?
It must be the purveyor; he had the power to purchase, and he ought to have been ordered to purchase.

Is not the purveyor an inferior officer in the hospital and has he the power to thwart and counteract the superior medical authority in the hospital?
He supposes that he has. I do not think he has; and supposing that he thinks that he has, he is able to do it as well as if he had it.

So that the primary cause of this suffering and misery must have been a conflict between the authority of the senior medical man in the hospital and the purveyor?
I can hardly venture to speak to that.

This conflict and uncertainty of authority in all the departments connected with the administration of the medical department of the army, and this timidity and hesitation on the part of every person in the establishment led to this great embarrassment?
Clearly. I will instance with reference to that, that until the war broke out, I had for 40 years been nursed to save money, and not to spend it; and when I found on this war coming on that the country was

liberal, and that I dared to spend money, I felt that the screw had been so tightly applied to me, that I could not believe myself when I knew that I could spend money without going through the regular forms; and it was months before I could convince myself that I had the power vested in me.

Have you brought the account of the medical comforts?
Yes, you asked for the original.

This paper is dated the 28th February 1855?
It should be 1854, it is an error of the clerk. And with reference to the clerk the pressure has been so great, that it is not to be wondered that a little mistake has been made.

Will you look at the paper?
Yes certainly.

There is the 24th January 1855; will you look at that; there are 60 pipes of wine, each pipe being 117 gallons?
Yes, they are gone out.

On the same day there were 1,400 dozens of port wine; will you be good enough to find that in those returns?
I would suggest, that instead of asking me these questions, the storekeeper, who has the whole charge of these things and can go into details should be questioned; because the general duties of the office have taken me 14 hours a day and I have not been able to go through every one of these.

Did you not make that return to the House of Commons, and is not your name signed to it?
My name is signed to this.

Are you not responsible for it?
Virtually I am; but at the same time those who make up the statement in the office are responsible.

Fourteen hundred dozens of port wine and 60 pipes on the same day are not such a small matter. I apprehend you have made a mistake in correcting those figures; the Committee want to know where you begin in dealing with your requisitions, and without casting imputation upon you, we must have these figures explained?
Clearly, most decidedly. I was never educated for stores, and this is a duty imposed upon me that was never imposed on any director general in the world; before leaving the room, I wish to say I hope for my sake, the matter be thoroughly probed.

You may depend upon that it will be; for the sake of the public.

. . .

Have you not been lately urged, or advised, or received some hint, that it would be well if you were to resign your office?
No, I have not; except so far as this, that I have been told that my health is breaking. I was perfectly aware of that myself, months and months ago, and I consulted a celebrated physician in London, upon the point, and told him that I had only one reason for not

going on as I was, 14 hours a day, feeling that I did not know what day I was to be laid upon my death bed. He said and urged it strongly, "You will have an opportunity of stating your case, and then I, as your medical man, strongly urge you to the course you have meditated."

I did not mean at all any private advice which you have received from your own medical attendant, but whether you had received any official hints from any superior of any sort or kind to that effect?
I have been told that the medical department of the army was to be reorganised; and I was told in what way it was to be reorganised; when I immediately said, "Then I must be allowed to retire from my position; I cannot hold that appointment when the reorganisation takes place." That was the only hint.

It has been represented to this Committee by competent witnesses, who have themselves seen the facts upon the spot, that nothing could be so horrible or so disgusting, or in every way so calamitous, as the state of those hospitals from the time of the arrival of the sick from the battle of the Alma, and for a considerable time afterwards. It has also been stated by Mr. MacDonald, the witness who was sent to distribute the charitable fund collected by "The Times" newspaper, that he applied to you upon the 5th of November for a letter of introduction, and for information with respect to the state of the hospitals in the East, and that you at that time told him, that his mission was a very supererogatory one, and not required at all, inasmuch as ample means had been provided, and that every precaution taken to supply every-thing that was necessary for the comforts and the care of the sick in the hospitals at Scutari; what reports had you at that time from Constantinople to justify that representation?

I had no reports that justified me in saying anything else.

There were very few beds; the poor soldiers were brought down with scarcely any clothes, their clothes having been worn off their backs, were placed upon palliasses, and their clothes, or at least the remnants of them, full of vermin, taken off their backs and put under the palliasses; no washing had been performed in the hospital, nor the floor washed for six weeks; no washing of linen had been performed; there were no hospital dresses; that there was neither cooking, nor com-forts of any kind provided; and as to the whole state of the hospital, it was pestiferous and infectious, the privies being in such a state that nobody could approach the place. This is the description that has been given before this Committee of the state of the hospitals at this time.

Table of deaths at Scutari and Kuleli hospitals.

June 1854	6
July	13
August	19
September	112
October	235
November	320
December	601
January 1855	1,393
February	1,476
March	555
April	201
May	46
Total 1854–1855	4,977

In January 1856, on account of the conduct of the war in the Crimea, the Government, including Lord Aberdeen, the Prime Minister and the Duke of Newcastle, the Minister of War, resigned.
Lord Palmerston became Prime Minister.

Documents used

House of Commons papers: No.449 August 1855; No. 123 March 1855; No.135 March 1855; No.156 March 1855; No. 2119 1856; C 1920 1855; No. 218 1855.

The Report of the Royal Engineers on the Siege of Sebastopol.

The Medical and Surgical History of the British Army in the Years 1854,5,6, 2434,Vol.2.

Other titles in the series

John Profumo and Christine Keeler, 1963

"The story must start with Stephen Ward, aged fifty. The son of a clergyman, by profession he was an osteopath ... his skill was very considerable and he included among his patients many well-known people ... Yet at the same time he was utterly immoral."

The Backdrop

The beginning of the '60s saw the publication of 'Lady Chatterley's Lover' and the dawn of sexual and social liberation as traditional morals began to be questioned and in some instances swept away.

The Book

In spite of the recent spate of political falls from grace, the Profumo Affair remains the biggest scandal ever to hit British politics. The Minister of War was found to be having an affair with a call girl who had associations with a Russian naval officer at the height of the Cold War. There are questions of cover-up, lies told to Parliament, bribery and stories sold to the newspapers. Lord Denning's superbly written report into the scandal describes with astonishment and fascinated revulsion the extraordinary sexual behaviour of the ruling classes. Orgies, naked bathing, sado-masochistic gatherings of the great and good and ministers and judges cavorting in masks are all uncovered.

ISBN 0 11 702402 3   Price £6.99

The Loss of the Titanic, 1912

"From 'Mesabe' to 'Titanic' and all east bound ships. Ice report in Latitude 42N to 41.25N; Longitude 49 to 50.30W. Saw much Heavy Pack Ice and a great number of Large Icebergs. Also Field Ice. Weather good. Clear."

The Backdrop
The watchwords were "bigger, better, faster, more luxurious" as builders of ocean-going vessels strove to outdo each other in their race to capitalise on a new golden age of travel.

The Book
The story of the sinking of the *Titanic*, as told by the official enquiry, reveals some remarkable facts which have been lost in popular re-tellings of the story. A ship of the same line, only a few miles away from the *Titanic* as she sank, should have been able to rescue passengers, so why did this not happen? Readers of this fascinating report will discover that many such questions remain unanswered and that the full story of a tragedy which has entered into popular mythology has by no means been told.

ISBN 0 11 702403 1   Price £6.99

Tragedy at Bethnal Green: 1943

"Immediately the alert was sounded a large number of people left their houses in the utmost haste for shelter. A great many were running. Two cinemas at least in the near vicinity disgorged a large number of people and at least three omnibuses set down their passengers outside the shelter."

The Backdrop

The beleaguered East End of London had borne much of the brunt of the Blitz but, in 1943, four years into WWII, it seemed that the worst of the bombing was over.

The Book

The new unfinished tube station at Bethnal Green was one of the largest air raid shelters in London. After a warning siren sounded on 3 March 1943, there was a rush to the shelter. By 8.20pm, a matter of minutes after the alarm had sounded, 174 people lay dead, crushed in their attempt to get into the tube station's booking hall. At the official enquiry, questions were asked about the behaviour of certain officials and whether the accident could have been prevented.

ISBN 0 11 702404 X   Price £6.99

The Judgement of Nuremberg, 1946

"Efficient and enduring intimidation can only be achieved either by Capital Punishment or by measures by which the relatives of the criminal and the population do not know the fate of the criminal. This aim is achieved when the criminal is transferred to Germany."

The Backdrop

WWII is over, there is a climate of jubilation and optimism as the Allies look to rebuilding Europe for the future but the perpetrators of Nazi War crimes have still to be reckoned with, and the full extent of their atrocities is as yet widely unknown.

The Book

Today, we have lived with the full knowledge of the extent of Nazi atrocities for over half a century and yet they still retain their power to shock. Imagine what it was like as they were being revealed in the full extent of their horror for the first time. In this book the judges at the Nuremberg Trials take it in turn to describe the indictments handed down to the defendants and their crimes. The entire history, purpose and method of the Nazi party since its foundation in 1918 is revealed and described in chilling detail.

ISBN 0 11 702406 6   Price £6.99

The Boer War 1900: Ladysmith and Mafeking

"4th February – From General Sir Redvers Buller to Field-Marshal Lord Roberts … I have today received your letter of 26 January. White keeps a stiff upper lip, but some of those under him are desponding. He calculates he has now 7000 effectives. They are eating their horses and have very little else. He expects to be attacked in force this week … "

The Backdrop

The Boer War is often regarded as one of the first truly modern wars, as the British Army, using traditional tactics, came close to being defeated by a Boer force which deployed what was almost a guerrilla strategy in punishing terrain.

The Book

Within weeks of the outbreak of fighting in South Africa, two sections of the British Army were besieged at Ladysmith and Mafeking. Beginning with despatches describing the losses suffered by the British Army at Spion Kop on its way to rescue the garrison at Ladysmith, the book goes on to describe the lifting of the siege. The second part of the book gives Lord Baden Powell's account of the siege of Mafeking and how the soldiers and civilians coped with the inevitable hardship.

ISBN 0 11 702408 2   Price £6.99

The British Invasion of Tibet:
Colonel Younghusband, 1904

"On the 13th January I paid ceremonial visit to the Tibetans at Guru, six miles further down the valley in order that by informal discussion I might assure myself of their real attitude. There were present at the interview three monks and one general from Lhasa. These monks were low-bred persons, insolent, rude and intensely hostile; the generals, on the other hand, were polite and well-bred."

The Backdrop

At the turn of the century, the British Empire was at its height, with its army at the forefront of the mission to bring what the Empire saw as the tremendous civilising benefits of the British way of life to those nations which it regarded as still languishing in the dark ages.

The Book

In 1901, a British missionary force under the leadership of Colonel Francis Younghusband crossed over the border from British India and invaded Tibet. Younghusband insisted on the presence of the Dalai Lama at meetings to give tribute to the British and their Empire. The Dalai Lama merely replied that he must withdraw. Unable to tolerate such an insolent attitude, Younghusband marched forward and inflicted considerable defeats on the Tibetans in several one-sided battles.

ISBN 0 11 702409 0   Price £6.99

War 1914: Punishing the Serbs

" ... I said that this would make it easier for others such as Russia to counsel moderation in Belgrade. In fact, the more Austria could keep her demand within reasonable limits, and the stronger the justification she could produce for making any demands, the more chance there would be for smoothing things over. I hated the idea of a war between any of the Great Powers, and that any of them should be dragged into a war by Serbia would be detestable."

The Backdrop

In Europe before WWI, diplomacy between the Embassies was practised with a considered restraint and politeness which provided an ironic contrast to the momentous events transforming Europe forever.

The Book

Dealing with the fortnight leading up to the outbreak of the First World War, the book mirrors recent events in Serbia to an astonishing extent. Some argued for immediate and decisive military action to punish Serbia for the murder of the Archduke Franz Ferdinand. Others pleaded that a war should not be fought over Serbia. The powers involved are by turn angry, conciliatory and, finally, warlike. Events take their course as the great war machine grinds into action.

ISBN 0 11 702410 4   Price £6.99